Bryant

SPECTRUM WRITING

CONTENTS

Project Editor: Sandra Kelley
Text: Written by Mary Waugh
    Design and Production by A Good Thing, Inc.
    Illustrated by Karen Pietrobono, Claudia Fouse, Anne Stockwell,
        Teresa Delgado, Doug Cushman

This book is dedicated to our children — Alyx, Nathan, Fred S., Dawn, Molly, Ellen, Rashaun, Brianna, Michele, Bradley, BriAnne, Kristie, Caroline, Dominic, Corey, Lindsey, Spencer, Morgan, Brooke, Cody, Sydney — and to all children who deserve a good education and who love to learn.

McGraw-Hill Consumer Products

Things To Remember About Writing

WRITING

- Be sure all sentences in a paragraph tell about one main idea.
- Use sequence words like *before* and *then* to tell the order of events.
- Add *er* or *est, more* or *most* to adjectives to compare things.
- Use exact details to make a description clearer.
- Use facts to make your writing more informative. Use opinions to tell how you feel.
- Organize cause and effect paragraphs by stating a cause and then describing the effects.
- Know your purpose before you begin to write.
- Decide on your point of view before you begin to write.

REVISING

- Use words that are exact to make your sentences clear.
- Combine short sentences to make your paragraphs smoother.
- Vary your sentence lengths; use some short sentences and some longer ones.
- Use only one point of view at a time.

PROOFREADING

Check to see that you
- used capital letters correctly
- punctuated sentences correctly
- used correct verb forms
- used correct plural forms
- said exactly what you wanted to say

McGraw-Hill
Consumer Products

A Division of The McGraw-Hill Companies

Send all inquiries to:
McGraw Hill Consumer Products
8787 Orion Place
Columbus, OH 43240-4027

ISBN 1-57768-144-4

6 7 8 9 10 POH 03 02 01

unit 1
Writing Main Ideas

Things to Remember About Using Main Ideas in Your Writing

The **main idea** of a paragraph is what the whole paragraph is about.

Writing
- Group sentences that tell about one main idea into a paragraph.
- Tell the main idea of a paragraph in a topic sentence.
- Make all the sentences in a paragraph tell about the main idea so that your paragraph is clear.

Revising
- Use exact nouns to make your sentences clearer and more interesting.

Proofreading Check to see that every sentence
- has a subject and verb
- begins with a capital letter
- ends with a period, an exclamation point, or a question mark

1 Grouping items

Imagine that you work in a supermarket. You have to put the pictured items on the shelves. How will you group them? You can put each one into a **category.** A category is a group of things that are alike. Each category belongs on a different shelf.

A. Read each category name below. Then write the name of each pictured item in the correct column.

Meats	Fruits	Cleaning Aids

B. The words in each list below belong to a category. Think of a category name, and write it on the line above each group.

_____   _____   _____

trout	quarter	birch
shark	dime	pine
goldfish	dollar	oak

C. Read each list below. Find the item that does *not* fit, and put a line through it. Then write a category name above each list.

_____   _____   _____

lollipops	canary	skating
lemon drops	cat	swimming
onions	rooster	basketball
jelly beans	sparrow	arithmetic

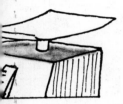

Copy each category below on a separate sheet of paper. Under each, write three or more items that fit the category.

Yellow Things	Things That Fly
Vegetables	Clothes

You can group items that are alike into a category.

lesson

2 Finding the main idea

Look at the picture.

A. Underline the sentence below that tells what the whole picture is *all* about.

1.   The piano player is holding her ears.
2.   No one likes the man's singing.
3.   There are tomatoes on the stage.

The sentence that tells what the whole picture is all about is called the **main idea.** The other sentences describe **details** in the picture.

B. One detail of the picture is the woman holding her ears. Write another detail of the picture.

_____

Paragraphs also have main ideas and details. A paragraph is a group of detail sentences that tell about one main idea.

4

C. Read the paragraph below. Pay attention to the detail sentences.

Marie pushed her carrots to one side of her plate. She flattened the top of her mashed potatoes and placed one carrot there. Then she cut her meat into small pieces. She put them in a circle around the mound of potatoes. "Aren't you going to eat, Marie?" her mother asked.

Now underline the sentence below that tells the main idea.

1. Marie pushed her carrots aside.
2. Marie's mother asked her a question.
3. Marie played with her food instead of eating it.

D. Read the next paragraph. Write two details from it. Then write its main idea.

What a day Mr. Montez had! First the car wouldn't start. Then he found two angry customers waiting for him at the store. About noon, he got a headache that lasted all afternoon. That night, his favorite TV show was replaced by a special on turnips.

Detail: _____

Detail: _____

Main Idea: _____

Think of a main idea, or choose one of these:

My pet is the smartest animal.
Summer is the best time of year.

On another paper, write a paragraph without stating the main idea in exact words. Make your detail sentences clear enough so that your readers will understand your main idea.

A paragraph is a group of detail sentences that tell about one main idea. The main idea of a paragraph is what the whole paragraph tells about.

---

3 Writing a topic sentence

Sometimes the main idea of a paragraph is stated in one sentence in the paragraph. This sentence is called the **topic sentence.** Topic sentence is another name for the main idea.

A. Read the paragraph below. Think about the main idea.

> She was the prettiest horse I ever saw. Her hide shone like a polished copper kettle. Her tail streamed in the breeze when she trotted, and she tossed her head proudly.

1. Draw a line under the topic sentence.
2. Write two details.

_____

_____

The topic sentence often comes at the beginning of a paragraph. But sometimes it comes at the end or even in the middle.

B. Read the next two paragraphs. Underline the topic sentence in each.

> Julio started down the stairs. He was careful not to walk on loose steps that might groan under his weight. His hand gripped the rail, but not too tightly. What if it creaked? Holding his breath, he tiptoed from step to step. Finally he stood in the dark at the bottom. Julio got to the basement without making a sound.

> My sister doesn't like the rain. But I think rainy days can be fun. We play card games for hours, and I usually win. We dress up in old hats and capes and pretend we're old-fashioned ladies. Most of all, I like to sit on the window seat and read while rain splatters on the windowpane outside.

C. The topic sentence in the next paragraph is missing. Add up the detail sentences to find the main idea. Then write a good topic sentence.

The burning sun rose higher over the city. People leaned out of windows and fanned themselves. Children sat limply on curbs. Ice cream and cold drink sellers were the only people

working. _____

_____

On another sheet of paper write your own paragraph. Choose one of the topic sentences below or think of your own. Try putting your topic sentence first. Then rewrite your paragraph, moving your topic sentence to another place in the paragraph.

I love to walk in the park in the spring.
Photos help me to remember good times.
My old sneakers have been good friends.

The topic sentence tells the main idea of a paragraph.

Writing sentences that keep to the topic

A. Find two details that *don't belong* in the picture above. Write them on the lines below.

_____   _____

In a picture, the details should all fit the main idea. The same thing is true of a paragraph. When you write a paragraph, make sure that all of your detail sentences tell about the main idea of your paragraph.

8

B. Read the following paragraphs. Underline the topic sentence in each. Then draw a line through each sentence that doesn't tell about the main idea.

1. What an exciting game we played last Saturday! The score was tied in the ninth inning with a runner on third. Donna came up to bat. She has red hair. Soon there were two strikes against her, and we were ready to call it quits. Then she hit the pitch well and beat out the throw. Our winning run scored.

2. The triangle-players went over their parts one more time. The first trumpet-player loosened up his lips with two runs up and down the scale. The kettle-drummer, testing for tone, tapped his big copper tubs quietly. Tickets to the band concert were quite expensive. The band members were getting ready to play.

3. Uncle Jake loves to make unusual sandwiches. One of his favorites is peanut butter, tuna, and banana on toast. Did you ever watch a monkey eat a banana? He almost always uses peanut butter on his sandwiches. He says it helps hold everything together.

Write a paragraph of your own. Choose one of the topics below or think of your own. Be sure that all of your detail sentences tell about the topic of your paragraph.

My Favorite Salad   Caring for a Pet
A Funny Dream   My Secret Hideout

All the sentences in a paragraph should tell about the main idea of the paragraph.

5 Writing paragraphs about special topics

Look carefully at the picture below. Think about the topic of the picture. Think about the details in the picture.

A. You already know that a paragraph is a group of detail sentences that tell about one topic. On the following lines, write a paragraph about the picture. But, *do not* write the main idea of the picture in one topic sentence. Instead, write enough detail sentences so that your readers will understand the main idea without a topic sentence.

_____

_____

_____

_____

_____

_____

_____

_____

B. Use the following topic sentence to write another paragraph:

I love (or hate) to get up in the morning.

Remember, you may place a topic sentence at the beginning or at the end of your paragraph. Make your paragraph at least five sentences long.

_____

_____

_____

_____

_____

_____

Write On Choose your own topic. Or you may want to write about one of these topics: Sports, Food, Holidays. Then think of a main idea, such as "My Favorite. . ." Write at least one paragraph. Use a topic sentence *or* make sure that your main idea can be understood without a topic sentence.

_____

A paragraph may be written with or without a topic sentence.

lesson

Writing more exact nouns

What makes sentences interesting and fun to read? One thing is the words a writer chooses. For example, the sentence below would be more interesting if it had more exact nouns.

The <u>animal</u> played a <u>game</u> with the <u>person</u>.

_____

_____

A. Rewrite the sentence in two ways on the lines above. Use more exact nouns for each noun that is underlined. Choose from the nouns below or think up your own exact nouns.

Animal: kangaroo, tiger, canary, dolphin
Game: tag, checkers, musical chairs, baseball
Person: rock singer, explorer, princess, dentist

B. Here are some other nouns. Think of at least three more exact nouns for each. Write them on the lines.

1. Bird: _____ _____ _____

2. Color: _____ _____ _____

3. Flower: _____ _____ _____

4. Sport: _____ _____ _____

5. Vegetable: _____ _____ _____

6. Building: _____ _____ _____

7. Furniture: _____ _____ _____

C. Choose the more exact noun to complete each sentence below. Draw a circle around the noun you choose.

1. I went into the (building, barn).
2. There were several (horses, animals) inside.
3. I brought a (vegetable, carrot) for each one.

D. Rewrite the paragraph below. Change the nouns that are underlined to more exact nouns.

    The <u>person</u> went into the <u>building</u> to buy <u>vegetables</u>, <u>meat</u>, and <u>fruit</u>. At the checkout counter, the <u>worker</u> gave her only a <u>coin</u> in change. "<u>Things</u> are so expensive," she thought, as an <u>expression</u> crossed her face.

_____

_____

_____

_____

_____

_____

 Look over the paragraphs you've written for the Write Ons in this unit. Choose one paragraph to rewrite. Change your nouns so that they are more exact.

Choose exact nouns to make your sentences interesting.

Proofreading

Writing complete sentences

A complete sentence tells at least one whole thought. Read each word group below.

Birds fly.
The bright red bird on that branch

The first word group above is a complete sentence because it has both a subject (Birds) and a verb (fly). The second word group is not a complete sentence. It has a subject but no verb.

A. Read each word group below. Write S next to each word group that is a complete sentence and put a period after it. Write NS next to each group that is not a complete sentence.

1. ____ Not all birds

2. ____ Ostriches and penguins can't fly

3. ____ Ducks and geese

4. ____ Fly in a V-shaped group

5. ____ Hummingbirds can fly backward

A sentence begins with a capital letter and ends with a period, an exclamation point, or a question mark. Study these sentences.

My pet ^is^ a canary named Tweet. ^H^he likes to sing late at night and early in the morning. Why can't ^he^ sleep more and sing less ^?^

The sentences on page 14 have been proofread. Proofreading means reading over what you have written and making corrections. Notice how the corrections were made.

B. Proofread the sentences below and correct them. Follow the sample on page 14. Be sure each sentence has a subject and verb and that it begins and ends correctly.

Do you like to fly I think planes are great. they can you all over the world in just a few hours How wish I were on a plane right now!

As you proofread your writing, check to see:
- **that every sentence has a subject and verb**
- **that every sentence begins with a capital letter**
- **that every sentence ends with a period, an exclamation point, or a question mark**

Post-Test

1. Read the items in each category. Cross out the item that does not belong.

   a. **Games:** puzzles, checkers, jump rope, wrench, baseball

   b. **Traffic:** truck, car, bus, billboard, motorcycle

2. Underline the main idea in this paragraph.

   Toga's nose twitched, and he quivered with excitement. He raced in circles, sniffing the grass and trees. Toga seemed to know it was the first day of spring.

3. Read this paragraph. Then underline the topic sentence that fits the paragraph.

   Tom's pizza is freshly made with pure ingredients. Each slice has a thin, crispy crust, lots of tomato sauce, and plenty of cheese. Also, the price is the lowest in town.

   a. Pepperoni pizza is not my favorite.

   b. A bubbly hot slice of Tom's pizza is the best buy in town.

   c. Tom's Pizzeria is next to the savings bank.

4. Write a paragraph about the topic sentence below. Write at least five sentences that support the main idea.

   Saturday morning is a special time of the week.

5. Proofread and correct the sentences below. Add words where they are needed.

   Mom finished third in the minimarathon we cheered her at the finish line. Only running for one year.

unit 2
Writing in Sequence

Things to Remember About
Writing in Sequence

Sequence tells what comes first, next, and last.

Writing

- Use sequence words like *before* and *after* to help you tell the order of events.
- Put sentences in proper sequence when you write about how something is done.
- Tell *who, what, when,* and *where* in news stories. Write the facts in sequence.

Revising

- Use more interesting verbs to make your sentences clearer and more lively.

Proofreading Check to see that you have

- capitalized all the nouns that need capital letters
- formed plurals correctly

Writing about pictures in sequence

Do you ever read comic books? Comic book picture stories are drawn in a special order. That special order is called **sequence.** Sequence tells what comes first, next, and last.

A. The pictures below are drawn in sequence. They tell *part* of a picture story. Think about what the pictures show. Then draw a picture in the last space to complete the story.

First   Next   Last

B. Now write three sentences that describe the pictures of the girl. Be sure to write your sentences in sequence.

First   _____

Next   _____

Last   _____

C. The pictures below are *not* in sequence. Put the pictures in sequence so that they show a story. Write <u>first</u>, <u>next</u>, or <u>last</u> under each correct picture.

_____ _____ _____

D. Now write three sentences that describe the picture story above.

First _____

Next _____

Last _____

On another sheet of paper, draw a picture story of your own. Use three or more pictures for your story. Then, under each picture, write a sentence that describes it. Be sure your pictures and sentences are in sequence. You may use one of the ideas below, or you may think up your own idea.

Flying a Plane
Making a Pizza
Scoring a Point in a Game

Sequence tells what comes first, next, and last.

2 Writing with sequence words

Look at the pictures.

Before

After

Certain words always tell sequence. They are called **sequence words.** *Before* and *after* are sequence words. Some other sequence words are *first, then, next, last,* and *finally.*

A. Read the next paragraph. Then underline the sequence words in it.

   Mel looked at the painting, first with his head tilted to the left, then with it tilted to the right. Next he tried squinting at the painting. Finally he decided the painting was okay if you liked smashed fruit.

B. The paragraph at the top of page 21 uses sequence words. But the *sequence of events* is backwards. Rewrite the paragraph on the lines below by starting with the first event and ending with the last event. Change the sequence words so that they tell the correct order.

The elegant Lester LeMouche strolled down the avenue to his favorite restaurant. Before that, he splashed aftershave on his jaw and threaded a rosebud through the buttonhole in his jacket. And before that, he got dressed. Earlier he showered and shaved. At first, he peered at his pocket watch and saw that it was dinner time.

_____

_____

_____

_____

_____

_____

_____

 On another piece of paper, write a paragraph about your future. Tell about your plans. Write about what you might be doing two years from now, five years from now, and ten years from now. Use sequence words and circle each sequence word that you use.

Use sequence words to tell the correct order of events.

3 Writing about activities in sequence

Are you one of those people who find it hard to get organized in the morning? Or do you follow a certain sequence?

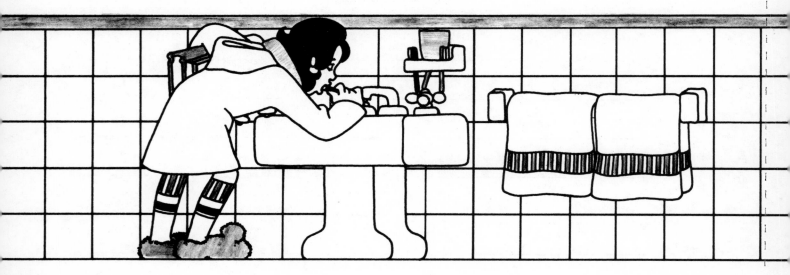

A. Here are some things most people do every morning. On the lines below, write them in a sequence that makes sense.

eat breakfast   put on a coat
turn off the alarm   get out of bed
get dressed   brush your teeth

First, _____

Second, _____

Third, _____

Fourth, _____

Fifth, _____

Last, _____

B. Imagine that while you're walking on the beach you see a bottle washed ashore. It has a message inside. What's the message? Write it on the line.

_____

Now think about where the bottle came from. Did it come from a boat, a desert island, a faraway land — or from your friend who likes to play jokes?

Write a paragraph about how the bottle got to the beach. Tell who wrote the message and when. Tell some details about the bottle's journey. Be sure your sentences are in sequence.

_____

_____

_____

_____

_____

_____

Write On What is your favorite game? How do you play it? Write a paragraph about the game using sequence words to describe how it is played.

_____

Be sure your sentences are in sequence when you write about an activity.

_____

Writing directions in sequence

A. The treasure map below shows where pirate gold is buried. Written directions are given at the top of page 25, but they are not in sequence. Using the map as a guide, arrange the six directions in the proper sequence by writing the correct numeral (1—6) beside each direction. The first two are done to get you started.

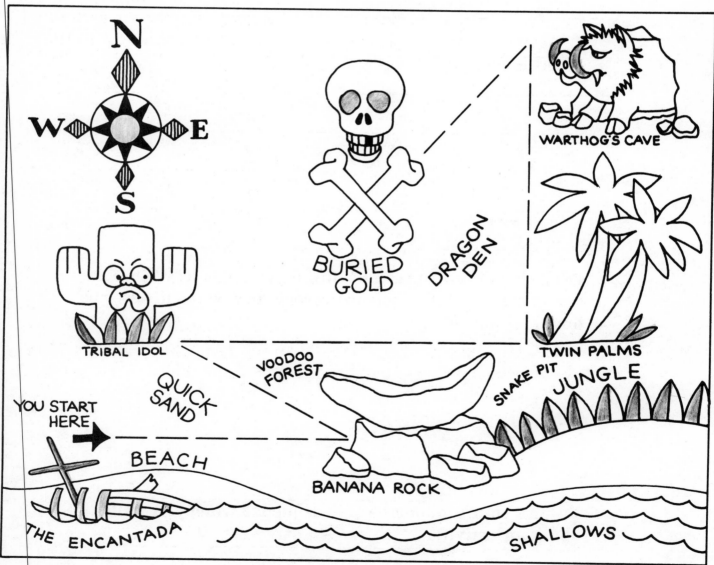

____ Eight paces north to Warthog's Cave.

____ Eight paces east to Twin Palms.

____ Four paces southwest. "**X**" marks the spot.

_1_ Start on the beach near the wreck of the *Encantada*.

____ Five paces northwest to tribal idol.

_2_ Six paces due east to Banana Rock.

B. Write directions that tell how to get from your classroom to the school cafeteria, office, gym, or some other location at school. Make each direction a complete sentence. Number your directions so that they are in sequence and so that a stranger to the school could follow them.

_____

_____

_____

_____

_____

_____

Write On Write a set of directions telling how to make a tuna fish sandwich. Or you may think up something else to write directions for. Make your directions complete and clear and put them in proper sequence.

Always write directions in sequence.

5 Writing a news story

A news story contains facts and events that answer the questions who, what, when, and where. The facts and events should be written in sequence.

Read the following news story. Think about what is wrong with it.

> New York, N.Y., May 26, 1977—____ Before he was halfway to the top, three police officers were lowered in a net to "rescue" him. ____ When he finally reached the top of the 1,350 foot building, he was arrested by the police. ____ George Willig, a 27-year-old toymaker from Queens, climbed up the side of one of the tallest buildings in the world early this morning. ____ Tomorrow he will have to pay a fine of one dollar and ten cents —one cent for each floor he climbed.
>
> ____ But Willig insisted on finishing the climb alone.

A. The writer has mixed up the sequence of events in the news story above. Put the story in proper sequence by writing the correct numeral (1—5) in the space in front of each sentence.

B. Play the role of a news reporter. Use the facts and events given below to write a news story on the lines. Be sure to put the facts and events in proper sequence.

Who: Dentonville Fire Team
When: June 3, 1979 — 9:52 A.M.
Where: Walter's Hardware Store, Olive Street
What: Trucks sent out; fire team fought blaze for two hours; Walter's store caught fire.

_____

_____

_____

_____

_____

_____

_____

_____

_____

_____

 Read the headlines below. Choose one that interests you and write a news story about it. Write your story in sequence and answer the questions who, when, where, and what.

Sea Monster Discovered in Local Lake
New Invention Makes Walking on Water Possible
Radio Messages Received from Planet Pluto

News stories tell who, what, when, and where. The facts should be written in sequence.

Revising

Writing with interesting verbs

lesson

Look at the picture and read the sentence below it.

Harry <u>went</u> up to the hurdle and <u>jumped</u> over it.

The underlined words in the sentence are verbs. Verbs express action. The verbs *went* and *jumped* tell something about what is happening in the picture. But these verbs could be more interesting. Read the next sentence that uses more interesting verbs to tell about the picture.

Harry <u>raced</u> up to the hurdle and <u>leaped</u> over it.

A. Read the following list of verbs. Then write two *more interesting* verbs for each one given. One is done to get you started. If you need help, use a dictionary.

look   *peek*   *glance*

1. talked _____ _____

2. ate _____ _____

3. walked _____ _____

28

4. went _____ _____

5. touched _____ _____

B. All of the verbs are underlined in the next paragraph. Using more interesting verbs, rewrite the paragraph. Use some of the interesting verbs that you wrote in part **A** or think up other interesting verbs.

Sam Spade <u>went</u> to the scene of the crime. He <u>looked</u> around for clues. Then he <u>walked</u> back to his office. He <u>ate</u> a sandwich quickly while he <u>moved</u> back and forth in the room. After a while, he <u>touched</u> his desk with his foot. He decided that his pet anteater had <u>taken</u> his hat after all.

_____

_____

_____

_____

_____

_____

 Now choose five sentences that you have written for this unit. Using more interesting verbs, rewrite the five sentences on another sheet of paper. Use your dictionary if you need help.

When you write, choose interesting verbs.

Proofreading

Writing nouns correctly

Most words that belong to categories are nouns. Here are some:

People	**Roads**	**Bodies of Water**
teacher	turnpike	lake
Mr. Goldberg	Poplar Street	Missouri River
Francesca	Jackson Drive	Atlantic Ocean

Notice that nouns that name specific people, roads, and bodies of water begin with **capital letters**. So do names of days, months, holidays, pets, cities, states, countries, and other special places.

A. Find the nouns in each category below that need capital letters. Write them correctly.

1. Days: thanksgiving day, wednesday, nice day

   _____

2. Animals: dog, rex, cat, mickey mouse

   _____

3. Places: desert, california, city, atlanta

   _____

B. Copy this paragraph. Replace each underlined word group with a name. Be sure to begin each name with a capital letter.

On <u>one day</u> in <u>a month</u> a boy rode down <u>the street</u>. He met his friend in <u>the park</u>. <u>The boy</u> and <u>his friend</u> swam in <u>the lake</u>.

_____

_____

_____

Most nouns can name one thing (singular) or more than one (plural). Singular nouns usually add *s* to make the plural form:

one kangaroo, two kangaroo<u>s</u>   one dime, two dime<u>s</u>

Nouns that end in *s, x, ch, sh,* or *z,* add *es:*

one sandwich, two sandwich<u>es</u>   one glass, two glass<u>es</u>

Nouns that end in *y* after a consonant change the *y* to *i* and add *es:*

one canary, two canar<u>ies</u>   one cherry, two cherr<u>ies</u>

Some nouns have irregular plurals. Others don't change:

one man, two <u>men</u>   one sheep, two sheep
one tooth, two <u>teeth</u>   one trout, two trout

C. Write the plural of each noun.

1. one opossum, two _____

2. one woman, two _____

3. one pony, two _____

4. one foot, two _____

5. one pitch, two _____

6. one hammock, two _____

7. one box, two _____

8. one deer, two _____

As you proofread your writing, check to see if:
- **you have capitalized all the nouns that you should**
- **you have formed all plurals correctly**

1. These directions on how to whistle are out of order. Number the steps in the correct sequence.

   _____ Blow air through your lips gently.

   _____ Shape your lips like an "O."

   _____ Make different notes by changing your breathing and moving your lips slightly.

   _____ If no sound comes, wet your lips and try again.

2. This paragraph describes going to a movie. However, some steps were left out. Rewrite the paragraph, adding the missing steps. Use sequence words like *first, next, last.*

   Marty and I checked the movie time in the *Daily Trumpet.* We handed our tickets to the usher at the door and pocketed our ticket stubs. Then we sat down to enjoy the buttery popcorn and the movie.

3. Change the verbs in the sentences to more interesting verbs. Write the new sentences on the lines.

   a. The lion <u>walked</u> through the long grass.

   _____

   b. The lion <u>jumped</u> at the zebra.

   _____

4. Proofread and correct these sentences.

   a. Jamie visited uncle ned in oklahoma city.

   b. We needed two boxs to put all the game away.

unit 3
Writing Comparisons

Things to Remember About Writing Comparisons

A **comparison** tells how things are alike or different.

Writing

- Add *er* or *more* to adjectives to compare two things.
- Add *est* or *most* to adjectives to compare more than two things.
- Use similes to make your writing clearer and more lively.

Revising

- Choose exact adjectives to make the meaning of your sentences clear.

Proofreading

Check to see that you have

- used a period to end a statement or command
- used a question mark to end a sentence that asks something
- used an exclamation point to end a sentence that shows strong feeling
- used commas to separate words in a series
- used commas to set off *yes*, *no*, and the name of a person spoken to

1 Comparing two things

The suitcase on the left is <u>lighter</u>.
The suitcase on the right must be <u>fuller</u>.

The sentences above are comparisons. Comparisons tell how things are alike or different.

Comparisons often use **adjectives.** Read the underlined adjectives in the sentences above. What two letters do they end in? ____ When *two* things are compared, the ending *er* is added to many adjectives.

A. Look at the pairs of pictures that follow. For each pair, write a sentence comparing the two things. Use the *er* form of the adjective given.

1.

fat: _____

34

2.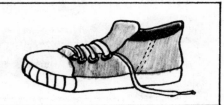

clean: _____

With longer adjectives, we use the word *more* to make comparisons: *more delicious, more beautiful.*

B. Finish each comparison below. Use words from the box, or think of your own adjectives. Use each adjective only once.

more expensive	faster	brighter
more playful	deeper	bigger

1. An apartment house is _____ than a cottage.

2. A kitten is _____ than a cat.

3. A car is _____ than a bicycle.

4. A lake is _____ than a puddle.

5. The sun is _____ than the moon.

 Choose one of the pairs below to compare. Make a list of *er* adjectives for each one in the pair. Then write three sentences, using the adjectives to compare the two things.

Sunday and Monday   a dog and a cat
a peach and a lemon   you and a friend

**A comparison tells how things are alike or different.
Add __er__ or __more__ to adjectives to compare two things.**

2 Comparing more than two things

Brenda is the <u>most skillful</u> skier on this hill.
She reached the bottom in the <u>fastest</u> time.

Read the sentences above. They compare Brenda to some other people. The adjectives used in the sentences are the words *fastest* and *most skillful*. When we compare more than two things, we add the ending *est* or use the word *most* with the adjective.

A. Write a sentence that uses each adjective below. Look at the picture of the skiers to give you some ideas.

1. coldest: _____

_____

2. most awkward: _____

_____

3. most difficult: _____

_____

B. Look at the three winners of the Centerville Dog Show. Write three or four sentences comparing the three. Use at least one adjective in each sentence. Here are some adjectives you may wish to use: *smallest, furriest, biggest, longest, most playful.*

_____

_____

_____

_____

_____

_____

Books of records often list the "most" and the "best." Make up your own list of at least six records. List things or people you think are the most or the best. Tell why you chose each one. Here are some to get you started.

Most delicious food   Most unusual hobby
Funniest person   Most useless object

Add <u>est</u> or <u>most</u> to adjectives to compare more than two things.

3 Writing comparisons correctly

You add *est* or *most* to an adjective when you compare more than two things. But how do you know which to add? With one-syllable adjectives and many two-syllable adjectives, use *est*:

dull, dull<u>est</u>   happy, happi<u>est</u>

Use *most* with long adjectives. Also use *most* with adjectives that end in *ful*, *ous*, *al*, and *ish*:

fortunate, <u>most</u> fortunate   careful, <u>most</u> careful

A. Read the paragraph below. In each sentence there is a choice of words in parentheses. Underline the correct form.

This part of the jungle was the (interestingest, most interesting). Snakes hung from the (lowest, most low) branches of the trees. Then we saw the (magnificentest, most magnificent) building we had ever seen. Surely this was the Temple of Bom Gabala, the (mysteriousest, most mysterious) temple in the world.

B. Remember to use *er* or *more* to compare two items. Use *est* or *most* to compare more than two things. Each label below contains two choices. Underline the word which correctly describes the pictured item.

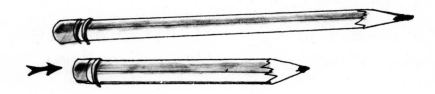

1.   the shorter/shortest pencil

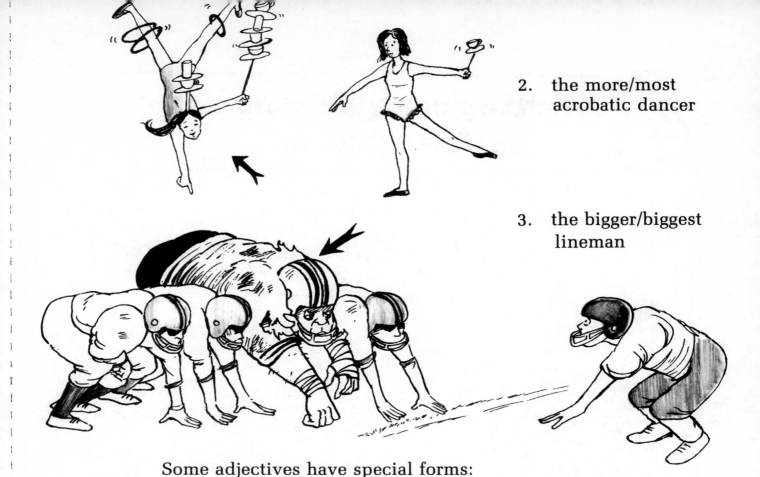

2. the more/most acrobatic dancer

3. the bigger/biggest lineman

Some adjectives have special forms:

good, better, best   bad, worse, worst

C. Write the correct form of each word in parentheses.

1. Arnie is a (good) _____ player than I am.

2. In fact, he is the (good) _____ player on the team.

3. Your yard looks (bad) _____ since you stopped mowing the lawn.

4. It is the (bad) _____ -looking yard on the block.

Use these adjectives: *noisy, comfortable, good, delicious, funny*. For each, write a pair of comparison sentences. In one sentence, compare two things. In the other, compare more than two. Be sure to write the adjective forms correctly.

When you write comparisons, be sure the forms of the adjectives you use are correct.

Writing comparisons with *like* and *as*

DAD LOOKS LIKE A FIRECRACKER ABOUT TO GO OFF!

Comparing Dad to a firecracker gives a clearer and more interesting picture than just saying he's angry. A comparison that uses the word *like* or *as* is called a **simile.** Similes can help make writing clearer and more lively.

A. Read these similes and answer the questions at the top of the next page.

    a.   My stomach feels as empty as a doughnut hole.
    b.   The stage was as bright as a million fireflies.

1. In simile a, the two things being compared are

   _____ and _____.

2. In simile b, the two things being compared are

   _____ and _____.

B. Now try writing some similes of your own. Complete the sentences below with the most expressive comparisons you can think of.

   1. At the sound of the starting gun, Elena ran as fast as

   _____

   2. When I shined Pa's old boots, they gleamed like

   _____

   3. The superjet stood on the runway, huge and shiny like

   _____

   You can describe something with several similes, making a simile poem.

C. Complete this simile poem.

   My striped scarf is as colorful as a field of tulips.

   Its wool feels soft, like _____

   It keeps me as warm as _____

   When I wear it, I look like _____

Write On Write your own simile poem. Choose something you own or something you see every day. Describe the object, using three or more similes, and see how unusual and interesting this everyday object becomes. Here are some things you might describe: a pet, a bike, a tree, a building.

A simile is a comparison that uses <u>like</u> or <u>as</u>.

Writing a comparison paragraph

Before you write a comparison paragraph, you may want to make a list of points to compare and words to use.

A. Look carefully at the two cars below. Then fill in the two columns below with words or phrases about each car. Use *er* or *more* adjectives, and any similes you can think of.

New Car	**Old Car**
_____	_____
_____	_____
_____	_____
_____	_____
_____	_____

B. Now write a paragraph comparing the two cars. You may wish to compare them point by point. Or you may wish to describe each one separately. Use the words you listed on page 42.

_____

_____

_____

_____

_____

_____

_____

_____

Write On What is your favorite food? Your least favorite? Which game do you love to play and which don't you like? What do you think are the best and worst books or TV shows? Choose a best and worst pair to compare. First list some words and phrases you want to use. Then write a comparison paragraph.

It is a good idea to make a list of comparison words before you write a comparison paragraph.

Revising

lesson 6

Choosing exact adjectives

SALLY IS WEARING A NICE SWEATER.

The sentence doesn't tell you much about Sally's sweater. Is it colorful, well-made, warm, soft? Adjectives like *nice* are not exact. Choosing exact adjectives can help make your meaning clear.

A. Each sentence that follows gives a choice of two adjectives. Draw a line under the one you think makes the sentence clearer.

1. That medicine tastes (odd, bitter).
2. The (bad, vicious) dog bit its owner.
3. We saw our breath in the (icy, cold) air.

4. Returning the money was the (good, honest) thing to do.
5. I like the beach on a (nice, sunny) day.
6. The figure in the dark cape seemed (mysterious, funny).
7. The golden, jeweled crown was (pretty, magnificent).

Instead of repeating the same adjectives in a paragraph, try using **synonyms.** Synonyms are words with almost the same meaning. You probably know many adjectives that are synonyms.

B. Each word in the first column below has a synonym in the second column. Draw a line to connect the two synonyms.

correct   tiny
awkward   peculiar
lucky   clumsy
little   fortunate
odd   right

C. Choose one picture in this unit that you like. Write a short description of the picture. Choose exact adjectives to describe the things in the picture.

_____

_____

_____

_____

_____

Write On   Look back at the comparison paragraphs you have written for this unit. Choose one paragraph to rewrite. Use exact adjectives and synonyms to make your comparison as clear and interesting as you can.

_____

Use exact adjectives to make your meaning clear.

Proofreading

lesson 7 Using punctuation marks

You know that every sentence begins with a capital letter and ends with a punctuation mark. But which punctuation mark should you use? Look at these examples.

Statement: Your suitcase is the same size as mine.
Command: Please weigh it for me.
Question: Why does it weigh more?
Exclamation: It feels like a ton of lead!

A. Answer these questions.

1. Which kinds of sentences end with periods?

   _____

2. Which kind of sentence ends with a question mark?

   _____

3. Which kind of sentence ends with an exclamation point?

   _____

B. Read each sentence below. Then put in the correct end punctuation mark.

1. What a tall building that is
2. How many floors does it have
3. It is the tallest building in the world
4. Can we go to the top
5. Push the button for the elevator
6. Here it comes
7. Whee   This is fun
8. Are we at the top yet

Commas are punctuation marks that help to make your writing clear. Here are two ways to use commas.

1. **Use commas to separate words in a series or list:**

   The smallest, furriest dog won the prize.
   That pear is the biggest, ripest, and juiciest.

2. **Use commas to set off the words <u>yes</u> and <u>no</u> and the name of the person you are talking to:**

   Yes, Jocko, you are the best dog here.

C. Add commas where they are needed in the sentences below.

1. Do you like to ski Lester?
2. Yes Jackie I do.
3. I like skiing skating and tennis.
4. Sports provide good healthful exercise.

D. Proofread this paragraph. Put in each missing capital letter, end mark, and comma.

the pond was a cool silvery mirror people skimmed twirled

and bumped to the ground the sounds of laughter and shouting

filled the crisp air was it a grand ball at the palace no it was only

Cooper Lake in the ice-skating season

Use a period to end a statement or command.
Use a question mark to end a sentence that asks something.
Use an exclamation point after a sentence that shows strong feeling.
Use commas to separate words in a series or list.
Use commas to set off <u>yes</u>, <u>no</u>, and the name of a person spoken to.

Post-Test

1. Write these comparisons correctly.

   a. more higher _____

   b. beautifulest _____

   c. curiouser _____

2. Complete these similes in any way you wish.

   a. The alarm clock rang like a _____.

   b. The new sports car was as sleek as a _____.

3. Write a list of words or phrases that compare a bird and a kite. Use the comparisons to write a paragraph.

bird	kite
_____	_____
_____	_____
_____	_____
_____	

4. Underline the more exact adjective in each sentence.
   a. Jody has (an unusual, a husky) voice.
   b. The apple pie had a (tangy, funny) taste.
   c. The sun on the beach was (hot, blistering).

5. Proofread and correct this paragraph.

   did you ever hear of an outer-space greeting card Many

   spaceships contain tapes pictures and other objects from Earth

   Scientists hope that intelligent beings will find these spaceships

48

unit 4
Writing Details

Things to Remember About Writing with Details

Details are small bits of information.

Writing

- Choose details that fit the topic.
- Use details to describe the way something looks, sounds, smells, tastes, and feels.
- Use exact details to make a description clearer and more interesting.

Revising

- Use adverbs and adverbial phrases to make your sentences clearer and more informative.

Proofreading

Check to see that you have
- used the *s* form of the verb with singular subjects
- used the plain form of the verb with plural subjects.

Writing details from pictures

Details are small bits of information. Details tell how things look, sound, smell, feel, taste, or seem. Exact details can make a description more interesting.

A. Read the paragraph below. Underline all the details you find. One has been done to get you started.

It was a <u>dry, hot</u> afternoon. An old, spotted pony came limping slowly down the dirt road. His thick hair was caked with dust. Suddenly, the tired animal stopped in his tracks. He saw a giant maple tree close by. Under the tree was a thick patch of grass. "What a great place for a little snack!" he thought.

Now put a check mark below the picture of the animal described in the paragraph.

1. ____   2. ____   3. ____

B. List four details you find in the picture on this page.

1. _____

2. _____

3. _____

4. _____

C. Now use your list of details to write a short paragraph about the picture.

_____

_____

_____

_____

_____

On a separate sheet of paper write a short description of a room in your home, including details. Then draw a picture of the room, showing each detail you've described.

Details are small bits of information. Pictures have many details.

2 Choosing details for a description

Something's strange about the picture on this page. What is an astronaut doing in the middle of a peaceful park? That detail doesn't fit the picture. A written description needs details. But you must choose details that fit the topic.

A. Read the paragraph below. Most sentences tell about a bowl of fruit. Cross out the sentences containing details that don't belong in the paragraph.

Eddie couldn't take his eyes off the bowl on the kitchen counter. It was filled with fresh fruit. He could see a bunch of plump green grapes, which were at their sweetest. Someone came in the back door and slammed it. Under the grapes were two fat pears. The dark gold color of the counter top shined. Filling part of the bowl were deep red strawberries dotted with drops of water. On top of this mountain of fruit was one perfect peach.

B. Suppose you are writing an ad for a snack food bar called Crinklies. Look at the list of details below. Write an **X** next to the details that would fit the ad. Then write an ad for Crinklies, using some of the details in the list.

____ crisp peanut butter coating

____ sharp as metal

____ thick and crunchy

____ makes teeth shine

____ filled with coconut and honey

____ colorfully wrapped

____ bite-size pieces

____ available at lumber stores near you

_____

_____

_____

_____

_____

Write On Write a description of a spooky house at midnight. You may wish to use some of the details below. Add your own details to complete the paragraph.

long, dark hall	creaking door	flickering light
strange tapping	ticking clock	shrill scream

Be sure your details fit the topic.

3 Describing with your senses

Your five senses can give you a lot of information. Imagine that you are walking through a county fair. Think of all the details you would see, hear, touch, smell, taste.

Even one sense can tell you a lot. Can you recognize someone by just hearing a footstep or a laugh, or smelling a special scent?

A. Write the name of the sense you would use most to notice each detail listed below. Choose sight, hearing, taste, smell, or touch. You may list more than one sense for each detail listed. One is done to get you started.

tangy orange juice ___taste___

a porcupine's sharp spines _____

puffy clouds _____

a creaking door _____

a turkey roasting _____

a silk shirt _____

peppery sausage _____

birds chirping _____

B. Imagine you are walking inside a deep cave. Your way is lighted by a single candle. Suddenly a drop of water from the roof of the cave puts out the candle. Write a paragraph about how you get out of the cave. You'll have mainly your sense of touch to guide you so be sure to include details about touch.

_____

_____

_____

_____

_____

_____

_____

Imagine you are a raccoon sniffing around a park. You come across a picnic lunch which is spread out on a blanket on the grass. No one is around. Write a paragraph with details describing all the delicious things you smell and taste.

_____

You can use details to describe the way something looks, sounds, smells, tastes, and feels.

55

Lesson 4 **Writing riddles**

What goes up when the rain comes down?

The question above is a riddle.* A riddle gives details that describe something but don't name it. Often the details are tricky. A good riddle can have only one answer.

A. Read each riddle below. Think about each detail. Then write your answer.

1. I am smooth and creamy. You store me in the refrigerator to keep me cold. You can eat me in a cone or dish. What am I?

   Answer: _____

2. I keep you from being late. I hang on the wall. Sometimes I make noises. I chime; I tick; I say, "cuckoo." What am I?

   Answer: _____

Notice how each new detail helps you to figure out exactly what is being described in the riddle.

*Did you guess that the answer is an umbrella?

B. Write a riddle. Choose one of the objects listed below. Be sure to use enough details so that only one answer is possible.

sand   rainbow   spaghetti   basketball

_____

_____

_____

C. Tricky riddles often use words, like _teeth_ or _hands_, that have more than one meaning. Look at the pictures and labels. Do they help you answer the riddles below?

1. What has many eyes but can't see? _____

2. What has teeth but never chews? _____

3. What has hands but no fingers? _____

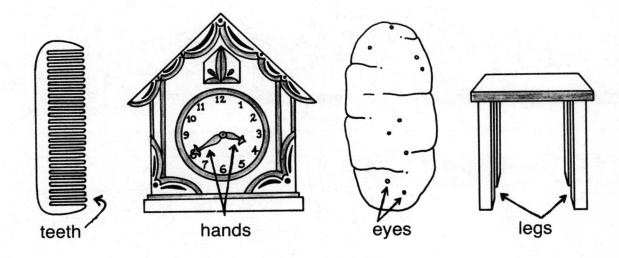

teeth   hands   eyes   legs

 On another sheet of paper, write a page of riddles—at least six. Use exact details. Make some of your riddles tricky. Use the pictures on this page to get you started. See if a friend can solve your riddles.

Details are important when you write riddles.

57

5 Writing detailed descriptions

You now know how important details are in riddles and pictures. You know that details in a description must fit the topic. You know that you get many details through your five senses.

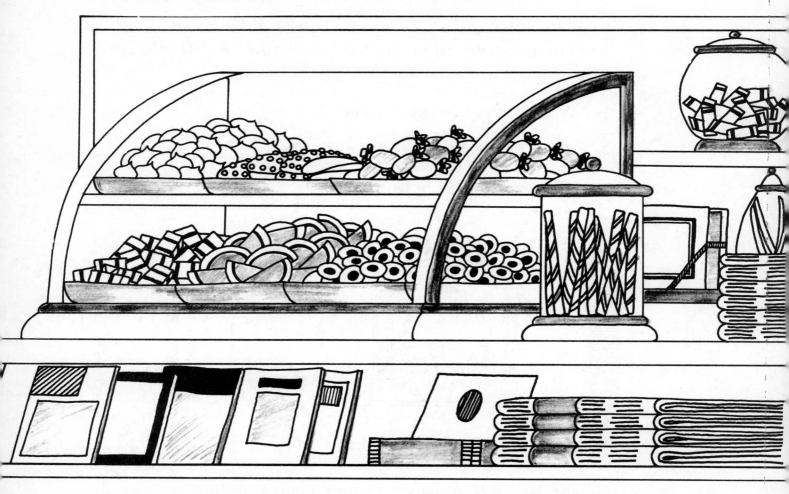

A. Use what you've learned to write a description of the items in the store pictured above.

_____

_____

_____

_____

_____

_____

_____

_____

B. Now make up your own details to describe a scene. Write a paragraph that describes a person sitting on the bank of a stream fishing. Try to include at least six details and refer to at least three of the five senses.

_____

_____

_____

_____

_____

_____

_____

 Think about your favorite store. Is it like the store pictured here? Or does it sell fruit, or baseball bats, or T-shirts? What special sounds and smells do you find in the store? What things do you touch and how do they feel? Write a description of your favorite store.

_____

Exact details can make a description more interesting.

Revising

Writing with adverbs

We went there then.
We went to the museum on Saturday afternoon.

Which sentence above gives you more information? Words like *there* and *then* are **adverbs.** They tell where and when. Word groups like *to the museum* and *on Saturday afternoon* are **adverbial phrases.** They tell where and when, but they give more exact details.

Here are some other adverbial phrases:

Where

under the bed
aboard the space ship

When

after the game
before next Tuesday

A. Replace each underlined adverb below with an adverbial phrase that gives more information. Write your new sentence on the blank line.

1. A mosquito flew <u>somewhere.</u>

   _____

2. The bus leaves <u>sometime.</u>

   _____

3. Let's go <u>there then.</u>

   _____

Lydia talked *excitedly* about the museum.

Adverbs like *excitedly* tell how. Many adverbs that tell how are formed by adding *ly* to adjectives.

excited + ly = excited<u>ly</u>   clumsy + ly = clums<u>ily</u>

B Change each adjective below into an adverb that tells how.

1. alert _____   4. quick _____

2. cautious _____   5. angry _____

3. fortunate _____   6. easy _____

C. Write a few sentences about the museum pictured on page 60, or a museum you like to visit. Try to use at least two how adverbs, and two when and where adverbial phrases.

_____

_____

_____

_____

_____

_____

_____

Write On Look back at the descriptions you've written for this unit. Did you use adverbs and adverbial phrases? Choose one description to revise. Add or change adverbs until your paragraph is as clear and interesting as you can make it.

Adverbs and adverbial phrases tell when, where, and how.

Proofreading

Using the correct verb form

Study the next group of sentences.

Philmore digs for roots.　　We gather mushrooms.
Rita hunts for eggs.　　　They cook chestnuts.

A. You already know that verbs are words that express action. What are the verbs in the model sentences above? Write them on the lines.

_____ _____ _____ _____

B. Now write answers to the following questions about the verbs in the model sentences above.

1. What two verbs tell about more than one person?

_____

2. What two verbs tell about one person?

_____

62

One verb form tells about a *singular* subject like "Philmore." Another verb form tells about a *plural* subject like "We." The singular form adds **s**. The plural form has no **s**.

C. Underline the correct verb form for each subject below. Then complete each sentence any way you wish.

1. Mom's car (run, runs) _____

2. Dad always (buy, buys) _____

3. We (like, likes) _____

4. The hamburgers (look, looks) _____

5. This pear (taste, tastes) _____

6. The runners (seem, seems) _____

7. Spot usually (hide, hides) _____

D. Write three or four sentences about something you like to do with a friend. Be sure to use the right verb forms.

_____

_____

_____

_____

_____

Use the s form of the verb with singular subjects.
Use the plain form of the verb with plural subjects.

Post-Test

1. Read this paragraph. Cross out the detail that does not belong.

   The Balloon Club met on a sunny, springlike day. Blue and silver balloons floated over the freshly mown field. I play softball there after school. My favorite was an enormous, silver, doughnut-shaped balloon that looked like a flying saucer.

2. Write five details about a Thanksgiving dinner. Use your five senses.

   a. taste _____

   b. sight _____

   c. smell _____

   d. sound _____

   e. touch _____

3. Use the details in Exercise 2 to write a paragraph describing a Thanksgiving dinner.

4. Underline the correct verb form in each sentence.

   a. Selma (goes, go) to ballet class on Thursdays.

   b. Most snakes (sheds, shed) their skins several times a year.

   c. Hank usually (plays, play) defense on the soccer team.

unit 5
Writing
Facts and Opinions

Things to Remember About
Writing Facts and Opinions

A **fact** is something that is true. An **opinion** is what someone thinks or feels.

Writing

- Use facts to make your writing more informative and believable.
- Use opinions to tell how you think or feel.

Revising

- Combine sentences by joining their subjects.
- Combine sentences by joining their verbs.

Proofreading
Check to see that you have
- put commas between the day and the year in a date
- put commas between the city and state in a sentence or address

Writing sentences of fact and opinion

Read the letter below.

Dear Sid,

Mom and Dad brought home my new bike yesterday.☐ It has racing stripes and a handlebar-mounted gear shift.☐ I think it would easily beat Eddie Blaine's bike in a race.☐ I bet it cost a lot more than Eddie's too.☐ Dad didn't tell me exactly how much my bike cost.☐ But I think it's the best-looking bike on the block.☐

Your friend,
Hiroshi

Some of the sentences in the letter are **facts.** Facts are sentences that are true. Other sentences in the letter are **opinions.** Opinions are what someone thinks or feels.

A. Read the letter again. Then write an **F** in each box that follows a sentence that is a fact. Write an **O** in each box that follows a sentence that is an opinion.

B. Look at the pictures.

Now write two sentences about each picture. Make one sentence a fact. Make the other sentence an opinion.

Fact: _____

Opinion: _____

Fact: _____

Opinion: _____

Fact: _____

Opinion: _____

C. On the lines below write three sentences that tell facts about your school.

1. _____

2. _____

3. _____

Now write three sentences that give your opinions about your school.

4. _____

5. _____

6. _____

On another sheet of paper write a paragraph of at least five sentences that are facts. Then write another paragraph of the same length that tells opinions.

_____
A fact is a sentence that is true. An opinion is what someone thinks or feels.
_____

2 Writing facts and opinions about different topics

Facts can be proved. For example, if someone says, "Ice melts when it is left at room temperature," it can be proved. Opinions usually can't be proved. For example, if someone says, "Fall is the best time of the year," there is no way to prove it. Opinions often have clue words like *think, best,* or *hate.*

A. Read the sentences below. Then write the word <u>fact</u> beside each sentence that can be proved. Write the word <u>opinion</u> beside each sentence that can't be proved.

1. _____ Some people are taller than I am.

2. _____ Hockey is the best sport of all.

3. _____ Spiders weave webs.

4. _____ Flying is the best way to travel.

5. _____ It's nicer to walk to school than to ride.

B. Write at least one sentence for each direction that follows. You may write more than one sentence for each one.

1. Write a fact about tomato juice.

   _____

   _____

2. Write an opinion about country music.

   _____

   _____

3. Write a fact about the governor of your state.

_____

_____

4. Write an opinion about watching TV.

_____

_____

 On another sheet of paper write three sentences that tell <u>facts</u> about what you see in the picture. Then write three or more sentences that tell your <u>opinions</u> of the picture. Your sentences of opinion might tell whether you like the picture, whether the picture is drawn well, or whether the picture tries to teach something. Or you may think of other ideas for your opinion sentences.

_____

Facts can be proved. Opinions usually can't be proved.

Writing about yourself in a diary

Read the following example.

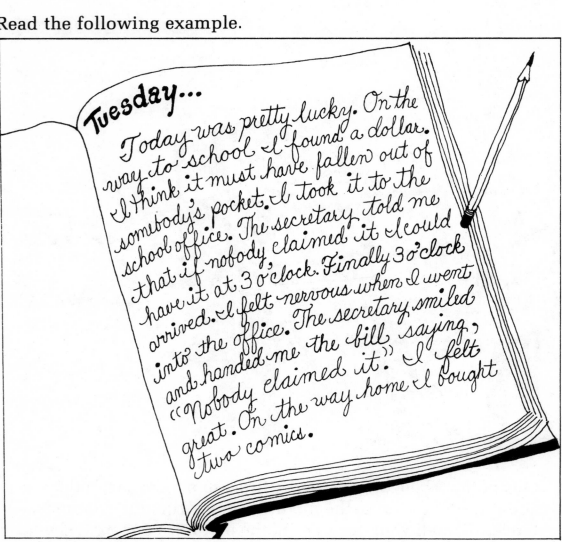

Tuesday...

Today was pretty lucky. On the way to school I found a dollar. I think it must have fallen out of somebody's pocket. I took it to the school office. The secretary told me that if nobody claimed it I could have it at 3 o'clock. Finally 3 o'clock arrived. I felt nervous when I went into the office. The secretary smiled and handed me the bill, saying, "Nobody claimed it." I felt great. On the way home I bought two comics.

The example above is part of a **diary**. A diary is a written record of what someone says, does, or experiences during a period of time.

A. Most diaries have both sentences of fact and sentences of opinion. Underline the sentences of fact in the example above. Then draw a circle around the sentences of opinion.

B. Now write part of a diary about yourself on the lines below. Write about the time between coming home from school and going to bed. In your diary, write both sentences of fact and of opinion. Make your diary at least six sentences long.

_____

_____

_____

_____

_____

_____

_____

C. Now, underline the sentences of fact in your diary. Then circle the sentences of opinion.

On another paper, write a diary for a whole week. Write the date for each time that you write in your diary. Remember to write both sentences of fact and sentences of opinion.

A diary is a written record of events in a person's life. A diary has facts and opinions.

lesson 4 Writing a sports paragraph

Read the following paragraph.

Yesterday I ran in the New York Marathon. The course was more than 26 miles long, and the race had over 11,000 runners in it! The day was too warm for a marathon race, but it was great fun just the same. Some of the runners tired early in the race. I think those who tired early didn't have enough practice. Anyway, I finished the race in about 4 hours. That wasn't the best time, but it sure wasn't the worst. The fellow who won the race had won it 2 years before too. His time was a little more than 2 hours.

A. Write answers to the following questions on the lines.

1. What sport is the paragraph about? _____

2. Where did the race take place? _____

3. How long was the race in distance? _____

4. Did the writer think the weather was perfect for the marathon? Why? _____

B. Look at the different sports pictured below. Choose two of the sports to write about. First write the name of each sport you choose. Then write two facts about each of the sports. Finally write two opinions about each sport.

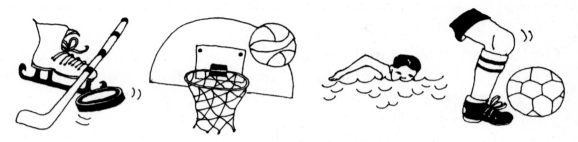

Facts and Opinions About Sports

Name of Sport: _____

Fact 1: _____

Fact 2: _____

Opinion 1: _____

Opinion 2: _____

Name of Sport: _____

Fact 1: _____

Fact 2: _____

Opinion 1: _____

Opinion 2: _____

On another sheet of paper write about a sport you think you might like to play as a professional. Write some facts about the sport. Write some opinions you have about the sport. Tell why you think you would be well suited to the sport you choose. Make your paragraph at least 8 sentences long.

Most writing has sentences of both fact and opinion.

5 **Writing a tall tale**

You know that facts are true and opinions are what someone thinks or feels. Well, there's another kind of statement. Think about the next sentence.

He drew a square circle on the board.

Everyone knows that there is no such thing as a square circle. That kind of sentence is false. Another kind of sentence that is false is the kind used in fairy tales. You have probably heard or read the following fairy tale sentence.

The cow jumped over the moon.

Sentences like the one above are often found in **tall tales** too. Tall tales are make-believe stories. But they are so hard to believe that they are usually funny. Tall tales are also called "whoppers."

Read the following tall tale.

On a farm one summer day in Kansas, a small boy went into a cornfield to get his family six ears of corn for dinner. He climbed

up to the top of one stalk to get the freshest ears. But the whole stalk was growing so quickly that the boy couldn't get down.

He called for help and his neighbor came running with an ax. But the cornstalk was growing so fast that the neighbor couldn't hit it twice in the same place. Then two farm hands tried to cut it with a saw but the saw got stuck and just grew away with the stalk. By that time the boy could no longer be seen. The stalk kept growing. To keep the boy from starving, his parents loaded a cannon with biscuits and beans and shot the food up to him.

A. Now write answers to the following questions about the tall tale.

1. Which is the first sentence that tells you that this story is going to be a tall tale? _____

   _____

2. Copy one sentence from the story that could be a true statement. _____

3. How did the boy's parents feed him? _____

   _____

 On another sheet of paper, write your own tall tale. Begin your story with a sentence that could be a fact. Then dream up a "whopper" and tell what happens. You may use one of the titles below or think up your own. Make your story at least five sentences long.

    The Strong Man Who Eats Rocks
    The Hottest Day Ever
    The Thin Woman
    The Biggest Mosquito

Tall tales are funny stories that are hard to believe.

Revising

Writing combined sentences

A. Read the next pair of sentences.

Billy left early.   Mark left early.

Write their <u>subjects</u> on the lines. _____ _____
The next sentence combines the pair.

Billy and Mark left early.

B. Read the next pair.

Sondra painted the fence.   Sondra cleaned the yard.

Underline the predicate of each sentence.
The next sentence combines the pair.

Sondra painted the fence and cleaned the yard.

When sentences are combined, sometimes their subjects are joined and sometimes their predicates are joined.

C. Now write <u>one</u> combined sentence for each pair of sentences below. Follow the examples above.

1. Carla called Ralph.
   Carla waved to Ann.

   _____

2. Maxine arrived at 6 o'clock.
   Sylvia arrived at 6 o'clock.

   _____

3. Susan walked three miles today.
    Karen walked three miles today.

    _____

4. Rodney reads a lot.
    Rodney writes a lot.

    _____

5. Duncan jumped out of bed.
    Duncan ran down the stairs.

    _____

6. The tiny squirrel peeped from behind the tree.
    The tiny squirrel scurried away.

    _____

7. The class ended.
    The class was dismissed.

    _____

8. Fryma prepared dinner.
    Fryma served dinner.

    _____

 Look back at ten sentences that you have written for this unit.
Combine the ten sentences into five sentences, and write your
five combined sentences on another sheet of paper. If you can't
find all ten sentences to combine, use the pairs of sentences
below.

Marge works hard.	Iris baked the cake.
Marge plays hard.	Iris frosted the cake.
Lynn swims well.	Laura went to lunch.
Lynn runs well.	Rosemaria went to lunch.

Combine sentences by joining their subjects or verbs.

Proofreading

Writing commas in dates and addresses

You use dates and addresses when you write letters. Sometimes you use them in regular sentences too. Notice where commas are used below.

251 Elder Street
Fort Wayne, Indiana
July 5, 1979 ← Heading

I was born on April 23, 1967.
My address is 125 Oak Place, Boulder, Colorado.

A. Fill in the answers below about the commas above.

1. In the heading of a letter, commas come between the day

   and the _____. Commas also come between

   the _____ and state.

2. Copy the date in the sentence: _____ .

3. In a sentence, a comma comes between the street and the

   _____ as well as between the city and state.

B. Put in commas where they are missing below.

1. Have you ever been to Dover Delaware?
2. The first men walked on the moon on July 20 1969.
3. Jonelle lives at 331 Baker Avenue Bangor Maine.

C. Write a heading for a letter. Use your home address and today's date. Put commas where they are needed. Then write a letter to a friend telling about something that happened to you this week. Remember to end your letter with a closing like "Your friend" and your signature.

_____

_____

_____

Dear _____ ,

_____

_____

_____

_____

_____

_____

_____ ,

_____

**Use commas between the day and the year in a date.
Use commas between the city and state in an address.
When you write an address in a sentence, put a comma
between the street and the city too.**

1. Read this paragraph. Then write **F** in front of the sentences that are facts, and **O** in front of sentences that are opinions.

    _____ The Wildcats beat the Cougars 8–3 on their home field last night. _____ The Wildcats played superbly. _____ They scored two runs in the first inning. _____ After that, they led throughout the game. _____ Timmy Hayes, the pitcher for the Cougars, seemed to lose heart near the beginning and played a dull game.

2. Write two facts and two opinions about your favorite book or TV show.

    Fact 1: _____

    Fact 2: _____

    Opinion 1: _____

    Opinion 2: _____

3. Combine each pair of sentences into one longer sentence.
    a. Chrissy built a sand monster.
        Ken built a sand monster.

        _____

    b. The elephant raised its trunk.
        The elephant roared.

        _____

4. Suppose your school decides to have shorter school days. But it also decides to stop summer vacations. Write a paragraph describing your opinion of these changes.

unit 6
Writing About Cause and Effect

Things to Remember When Writing About Cause and Effect

A **cause** sentence tells why something happened. An **effect** sentence tells the thing that happened.

Writing

- Use words and word groups like *so, because,* and *as a result* to join cause sentences with effect sentences.
- Organize cause and effect paragraphs by stating a cause and then describing the effects.

Revising

- Combine short, choppy sentences into one sentence to make your paragraphs smoother.

Proofreading Check to see that you have

- used an apostrophe and an *s* to make a singular noun possessive
- used an apostrophe to make a plural noun that ends in *s* possessive
- used an apostrophe to show where letters are left out in a contraction

Writing cause and effect sentences

Jenny's bike ran over a nail. So she got a flat tire.

These sentences express **cause and effect.** The first sentence tells a **cause**—a reason why something happened. The second sentence tells an **effect**—the thing that happened as a result of the cause.

A. Look at the picture on this page. Use it to help you write a cause for the effect listed below.

_____

That's why there are nails on the ground.

B. Read the cause and effect sentences on the next page. Match each cause and effect by writing the letter of the correct effect next to each cause.

_____ 1. Grandma is coming to visit.

    a. That's why his face is red and peeling.

_____ 2. Sheldon was out in the sun too long.

    b. Therefore, the tulips haven't come up yet.

_____ 3. I just ate fourteen ears of corn.

    c. So we're making up the bed in the guest room.

_____ 4. We've had a cold spring.

    d. As a result, my stomach doesn't feel so good.

C. Read each sentence below. It gives a cause or an effect. The other sentence in the pair is missing. Write a related cause or effect. One is done to show you how.

I forgot to put the ice cream in the refrigerator.

So it melted all over the counter.

1. _____ .

   Did my feet hurt!

2. Our TV set broke down last night. _____

_____ .

3. _____ .

   So I ate it with a spoon.

Write On

Do you remember facts and opinions from the last unit? On another sheet of paper, write three cause and effect sentence pairs. In each one, make the cause sentence a fact and the effect sentence an opinion. Here is a sample:
The moon is closer to earth than any planet. Therefore, I think we should start a moon colony.

In cause and effect writing, one sentence gives the cause or reason and the other sentence tells the effect or what happened.

2 Writing with cause and effect words

You may have noticed in the last lesson that certain words and phrases join causes and effects. Look at the underlined words below.

My bike has a flat tire. <u>So</u> I'll walk to school.
The vase broke <u>because</u> the cat knocked it over.

Words like <u>so</u>, <u>because,</u> <u>since,</u> <u>therefore</u> can join cause and effect sentences.

A. Underline the cause and effect words in the paragraph below.

> Since you're going to the flea market, I won't go. Everything sold there is always old and dusty. As a result, I start to sneeze. Once, because of my sneezing, I dropped a glass I was holding. Due to the fact that it broke, I had to pay for it. Therefore, I always stay as far as I can from flea markets.

B. Spaces are left blank in the sentences below for you to fill in cause and effect words. Try to use a different one for each sentence.

1. I'm sad _____ my goldfish died.

2. We ran out of milk, _____ we drank orange juice.

3. _____ so many people now enjoy tennis, the park is adding four new courts.
4. I was so full I couldn't even finish my vegetables.

   _____ I ate only two desserts.

C. In the space below, write a description of what is happening in the cartoon. Use cause and effect words.

_____

_____

_____

_____

_____

On another piece of paper, write at least five sentences about what you did and felt yesterday. Use cause and effect words wherever possible. Then underline each cause and effect word that you use.

Words and word groups like <u>so</u>, <u>because</u>, and <u>as a result</u> are used to join cause and effect sentences.

lesson 3 — Writing a cause and effect paragraph

Cause and effect is one way to organize a paragraph. You begin by stating a cause. Then you give the effects that come from the cause.

A. Read this paragraph and answer the questions that follow.

> We had more snow than usual last winter. Children missed so many days of school that they had to skip spring vacation to make up the time. Many businesses had to close down for several days because workers couldn't get in. Some people began to run low on food. But some people were happy. Snowmobile sellers, skiers, those who earn money shoveling snow, and those who just love snow had the best time ever.

1. What is the *cause* in the paragraph above?

_____

2. List three *effects* stated in the paragraph.

a. _____

b. _____

c. _____

B. Below is the opening sentence of a paragraph, with the rest left blank for you to fill in. Write what you think the effects will be as a result of the cause that is described in the first sentence.

    We had just set up all the food for our picnic when we saw a big brown bear coming toward us from the woods.

_____

_____

_____

_____

_____

_____

Write On Choose one of the causes below. On a separate paper, write a paragraph that tells what effects could result. Make your paragraph at least five sentences long.

a blackout   a misprint in a recipe   a landslide

You can organize a paragraph by stating a cause and then describing the effects.

Writing endings for story problems

The people in the picture have a problem. **Solving** a problem means telling how the problem is worked out.

A. Choose the ending below that solves the problem in the best way. Put an **X** next to the best ending.

_____ 1.   The tracks will never meet. So each set will continue to the other end of the country.

_____ 2.   The engineer will have each group of workers re-lay part of the tracks so that they meet.

_____ 3.   The engineer will fire all the workers, and everyone will go home.

In a way, a problem is like a cause. To solve it, you think of the possible effects and choose the one that works best.

B. Read each problem below. Then write your own ending. Choose the best way you can think of to solve the problem.

1. Just as Phyllis slipped her letter through the out-of-town slot at the post office, she realized that she had forgotten to

   put a stamp on the envelope. So _____

   _____

   _____

   _____

   _____

2. Mr. Brannigan was walking along the street when he saw an envelope. As he picked it up, he saw that it was full of money. There was no name or address on the envelope. So

   _____

   _____

   _____

   _____

   _____

Write On
Pick a real event in history, and write a paragraph about it. But add a make-believe problem to the story, and tell how the problem was solved. Here are some problems you might use:

What if Columbus's ships had termites?
What if Paul Revere's horse went lame?
What if Betsy Ross had no blue cloth to make the flag?

In one kind of paragraph, you state a problem and tell how it is solved.

Writing news stories that tell why

News stories tell **who, what, when,** and **where.** They also often tell **why.** These are sometimes called the "five W's."

A. Read the beginning of the news story below. Then write the "five W's" from the story on the lines.

> Mackerel, March 18. The Fish Fanciers Club of Mackerel held a giant festival today at the town dock. The purpose of the festival was to "get the country thinking about the important role played in our daily life by fish," said club president Shadroe McGill.
>
> The festival featured a parade, a poetry contest, and also

Who is the story about? _____

What happened? _____

When did it happen? _____

Where did it happen? _____

Why? _____

_____

B. Suppose you saw a news picture like the one above. Write a short news story to go with the picture. Be sure to include the five W's and tell why the event happened.

_____

_____

_____

_____

_____

_____

 On another sheet, write a news story of your own. Include all five W's. Here are some topics you might choose:

New Zoo Will Have No Cages
Person Given Medal by Mayor
Class Puts on Show

News stories tell who, what, when, and where. They also often tell why.

Revising

More about combining sentences

The ball is heavy.   The ball fell on my foot.

These two short sentences can be joined, or combined, to make one longer sentence. To combine sentences like these, you must be sure the subject of each sentence is the same.

Now look at the sentence which has a form of *be* followed by an adjective. This sentence can be made into a noun phrase. Here is how:

The ball ~~is~~ heavy.   The heavy ball

The *be* word is crossed off, and the adjective is moved to a place in front of the noun.

A. Now you try it. Change each sentence below into a noun phrase. Follow the example above.

1. The patient was nervous. _____

2. The dentist was eager. _____

3. The tooth has been painful. _____

When you have a noun phrase, you can put it in place of the subject of the other sentence, like this:

~~The ball~~ fell on my foot. (The heavy ball →
The heavy ball fell on my foot.

B. Now you try it. Use the noun phrases you made in **A.** Put them in place of the subjects of the sentences below. Write the new sentence you make. Follow the example.

1. The patient clutched his chair. _____

   _____

2. The dentist grabbed her tools. _____

   _____

3. The tooth was soon out. _____

   _____

C. Read the next paragraph. Can you find two pairs of short, choppy sentences to combine? Rewrite the paragraph, combining the sentences on the lines below.

   The cat was black. The cat howled on the back fence. The man was angry. The man threw his shoe at the cat. That woke everyone up.

_____

_____

_____

_____

Write On

Look back at the paragraphs you've written in this unit. Find some short, choppy sentences to combine. Choose one paragraph to rewrite. Combine the sentences to make your paragraph smoother.

You can sometimes combine two short, choppy sentences into one longer, smoother sentence.

Proofreading

Using apostrophes correctly

Jenny's bike ran over a nail.   Isn't that a shame?

Each sentence above contains an **apostrophe.** Apostrophes are used in two ways: to form **possessives** and to form **contractions.**
A possessive noun shows ownership:

the bike that Jenny owns = Jenny**'s** bike
the nails the workers have = the workers**'** nails

A. Write answers to the questions below.

1. To make a singular noun like *Jenny* into a possessive, you

   add _____ .

2. To make a plural noun that ends in *s* like *workers* into a pos-

   sessive, you add _____ .

B. Write each phrase below as a possessive phrase with an apostrophe. One has been done to show you how.

the parrot my cousins have =   *my cousins' parrot*

1. the cocoa the baby has = _____

2. the instruments that the musicians own = _____

   _____

3. the yells of the fans = _____

4. the boots that belong to the fire fighter = _____

   _____

5. the room for teachers = _____

Contractions are formed by combining two words and leaving out letters. An apostrophe is used to show where the letters are left out. Look at these contractions:

is not   isn't   you will   you'll

does not   doesn't   he is   he's

C. Write answers to the questions below.

1. When contractions are formed with <u>not</u>, the letter that is left out is _____ .

2. Contractions with <u>will</u> leave out _____ .

3. Contractions with <u>is</u> leave out _____ .

D. Make each pair of words below into a contraction. Don't forget the apostrophe.

1. could not _____   4. they will _____

2. are not _____   5. she is _____

3. I will _____   6. it is _____

E. Put in apostrophes where they are needed below.

1. Isnt Alans new camera nice?

2. Hes taking pictures of the school play.

3. Doesnt he have pictures of all the actors costumes?

Use an apostrophe and an <u>s</u> to make a singular noun possessive.
Use an apostrophe to make a plural noun that ends in <u>s</u> possessive.
Use an apostrophe to show where letters are left out in a contraction.

Post-Test

1. Complete these sentences by adding the word *therefore* or *because*.

   a. Fran couldn't find her sock _____ her dog ate it.

   b. The sky looks dark; _____ I will bring an umbrella.

2. Choose the best cause sentence for the following effect.

   Effect: The window was broken.

   a. The room is getting chillier.
   b. Tina and Sam played handball in the living room.
   c. The rain will ruin the furniture.

3. This news story is missing a *where* and a *when*. Read the story. Then add your own *when* and *where* sentences below.

   Lisa and Jeff Stein discovered part of a sailing ship while they were swimming. The wreck was a Spanish ship that sank over 300 years ago. Divers are now exploring the area to see if the entire ship can be uncovered.

   where _____

   when _____

4. Imagine that your town had a power failure. There was no electricity for two days. Think about five effects. Write about them in a paragraph. Include a topic sentence stating the cause.

unit 7

Making Your Point in Writing

Things to Remember About Making Your Point in Writing

The **purpose** of a piece of writing may be to entertain, inform, or persuade.

Writing

- Know your purpose before you begin to write.
- Use plus or minus words when you write to persuade.
- Write book reviews that inform and give opinions. Give reasons to support your opinions.

Revising

- Avoid choppiness in your writing by varying the kinds of sentences. Use some short ones and some longer ones.
- Join sentences properly. Correct run-on sentences.

Proofreading

Check to see that you have
- spelled the past tense forms of verbs correctly

Writing for a purpose

When we write something, we have a **purpose** in mind. We write stories, poems, and jokes to **entertain** our readers. We write directions or articles of fact to **inform** our readers. In letters or articles, we sometimes try to **persuade** people to act or feel a certain way.

A. Read each item below. Under it, tell whether its main purpose is to <u>entertain</u>, <u>inform</u>, or <u>persuade</u>.

1. People should eat more bananas. Bananas taste good and are good for you. Their skins keep them clean. Eat a banana a day to keep the doctor away.

   Purpose: _____

2. May: What kind of shoes do you make from banana skins?
   Ray: Slippers.

   Purpose: _____

3. Banana Shake
   Put one peeled, chopped banana in a blender. Add milk and one scoop of your favorite ice cream. Blend for one minute. Pour into a glass and enjoy.

   Purpose: _____

B. Think about the moon. Do you know any stories, jokes, or poems about it? Can you give some information about the moon? Could you persuade someone to go to the moon? Write a few sentences about the moon on the lines below. Under your sentences, tell your purpose for writing them.

_____

_____

_____

_____

_____

Purpose: _____

 On another sheet of paper, write a letter to a friend. Have three paragraphs in your letter. In the first paragraph, <u>inform</u> your friend about something you've learned or done. In the second paragraph, <u>entertain</u> your friend with a story, joke, or poem. In the last paragraph, try to <u>persuade</u> your friend to do something.

We write for a purpose. We write stories, jokes, and poems to entertain. We give directions and facts to inform. Sometimes we try to persuade someone to act or feel a certain way.

lesson 2 Writing to persuade

A. Suppose you want to persuade a friend to come out and play softball with you. Do you think you will have better luck if you say the things in paragraph 1, below, or the things in paragraph 2? Circle the numeral of the paragraph that you think is more persuasive.

1. We could go play some softball, I guess. I can't think of anything else, particularly. Some people think it's boring for two people to practice pitching and hitting, but it probably isn't so bad, maybe. You can pitch and go chase all the fly balls. You might as well come because I asked everyone else and you're the only one who isn't busy.

2. Super day for batting a softball, isn't it? I've got this new hardwood bat. I bet you can hit the ball farther than you ever did before with this bat. When you get a solid hit, you hear the noise go CRACK! We'll take turns chasing the ball, okay? Maybe we can get a soda afterward. What do you say?

B. Think about why paragraph 2 is more persuasive. Then list three things the speaker says in paragraph 2 that might make a listener want to come out and play.

1. _____

2. _____

3. _____

C. Often, when we write, we want to persuade the reader to have some particular feeling, desire, or opinion. Suppose you want to make a reader feel sorry for you because you have a lot of work to do. Write a paragraph on the lines below in which you try to make the reader feel sorry. Think about the details you should include. You might mention the time you must spend on the work, the kind of work, things you have to miss in order to do the work. Think, and then write.

_____

_____

_____

_____

_____

_____

_____

Write On On another sheet of paper, write a paragraph that tries to persuade the reader to swallow a spoonful of vinegar. Use words and details that make the vinegar seem desirable. Make your paragraph at least five sentences long.

When you write to persuade, think carefully about what to say.

3 Writing an ad

Anyone who wants to use words to persuade needs to have a feel for **plus** and **minus words.** Plus words are words that make us think of excitement, pleasure, and good feelings. Read the following ad-style paragraph. The underlined words are plus words.

> Now, you can have a <u>dazzling</u>, <u>radiant</u> <u>smile</u>. You can give your <u>dear</u> ones the <u>loveliest</u> <u>present</u> of all—a <u>happy</u> face that belongs to a <u>cheerier</u>, <u>bubblier</u> you!

A. Read the next paragraph. Then underline the plus words in it.

> Suddenly, a springtime-fresh new world of enjoyment opens up to you! Get to know the bright, happy taste of Jolli-Mints. They taste like laughter squeezed lovingly into a mint!

B. Minus words are just the opposite. They're the words that make you think of unpleasant things—pain, discomfort, ugliness, and bad feelings. Underline the minus words in the following paragraph.

> Fire damage is something no one likes thinking about. But here at Interstate Insurance, we want you to consider the grim, terrible facts. Your business could be ruined—you could lose thousands of dollars—if fire strikes. Don't be left sick, sad, and broke. Call Interstate!

C. Look at the pictures below.

First write a paragraph <u>full</u> <u>of</u> <u>minus</u> words about the baggy socks shown at left. Then write a paragraph <u>full of</u> <u>plus</u> <u>words</u> about the well-fitting socks on the right. A beginning for each paragraph is filled in to get you started.

1. Those saggy-baggy old horrors you see on the left are ＿＿＿

＿＿＿＿＿＿＿＿＿＿＿＿＿＿＿＿＿＿＿＿＿＿＿＿＿＿＿

＿＿＿＿＿＿＿＿＿＿＿＿＿＿＿＿＿＿＿＿＿＿＿＿＿＿＿

2. But those smart, sleek, super-stylish items gracing the legs

on the right are ＿＿＿＿＿＿＿＿＿＿＿＿＿＿＿＿＿＿＿

＿＿＿＿＿＿＿＿＿＿＿＿＿＿＿＿＿＿＿＿＿＿＿＿＿＿＿

＿＿＿＿＿＿＿＿＿＿＿＿＿＿＿＿＿＿＿＿＿＿＿＿＿＿＿

Pretend you're writing an ad for shampoo. On another sheet of paper write a paragraph full of plus words, describing what happens when the reader uses the shampoo. Then write a paragraph full of minus words, describing what happens if the reader doesn't use the shampoo.

Ads try to persuade by using plus or minus words.

Writing a business letter

Read the letter below. Notice the spacing and form of the letter. Notice also the names of the parts of the letter.

Heading

18 East Maple Street
Skellytown, Tx. 79088
April 10, 19___

Receiver's Address

Raoul's Plant World
627 Greenwood Avenue
Cherryville, Mn. 04622

Greeting

Dear Raoul:

Body

I am most interested in the man-eating plant that you have for sale. Please send me your complete plant catalogue so that I can read all about it. If I think I can handle the man-eater, I'll send you the list price plus the shipping charge in about a week.

Closing

Sincerely,

Signature

Roberta Bentley

A. Write answers to the following questions.

1. Besides trouble, what is Roberta Bentley asking for?

   _____

2. Where is the receiver's address written — on the right or the

   left side of the page? _____

3. What two things are included in the heading? _____

   _____

4. What is the closing? _____

5. What is the greeting? _____

6. What punctuation mark follows the greeting?

   _____

7. In what part of the letter is the purpose expressed?

   _____

Pretend you have one million dollars. Write a business letter that orders something or many things that you want. Or you may decide to give the money away. In that case write your letter to someone you would like to receive your generous gift. Follow the form of the business letter on page 104.

Business letters have a standard form. Business letters have an exact purpose.

5 Writing a book review

Read the following short book review:

Arthur's Artichoke is about a young man who plants an artichoke. (An artichoke, by the way, is a green vegetable that looks something like a tulip with lots of petals.) Arthur's artichoke is not ordinary though. It grows to giant size, about the size of a house.

However, the book fails to amuse or to arouse interest. So little information is given about the main character that readers get no clear idea of who he is or what he is like. Not only that, the author never completely lets us know what Arthur's feelings are about the growth of the giant artichoke. So we cannot clearly tell whether the ending is a great joy to Arthur or just a mildly interesting experience. The illustrations are attractive, and some of the language is catchy, but in general the author does not succeed in making us care about the book's outcome.

A. Write answers to the questions that follow.

1. Does the reviewer tell anything about the story of the book?

_____

_____

2. Does the reviewer think the book is good or bad? _____

_____

3. What are two reasons the reviewer gives for his opinion?

a. _____

_____

b. _____

_____

B. Now you try writing a short book review. Make yours a *favorable* review, one about a book you like. It may be either about a real book you have read or about an imaginary book, like *Arthur's Artichoke*. Whether it's about a real book or not, offer reasons to support your opinion that the book is good.

_____

_____

_____

_____

_____

_____

_____

Write On Now on another sheet of paper, write a short review of a book or story that you *have* read. Along with your opinions of the book, make sure you tell something about the story. Also, give reasons to support your opinions. Make your review at least two paragraphs long.

Book reviews inform. Book reviews give opinions.

Revising

Writing with rhythm

You probably know that poetry has **rhythm.** Rhythm in poetry is the regular beat or pulse.

Well, other forms of writing should have rhythm too. Rhythm makes writing smoother and more interesting to read.

A. Read the following example. Think about its rhythm as you read. Then write answers to the questions below.

After eating a pizza and seeing a movie that was about flying saucers, except not the scary kind, my sister and I went home then we decided to draw pictures about the stuff in the movie, only there were no pencils because my brother had taken them all, which is something he's always doing. I guess he was unhappy because we didn't take him to the movie, which was about flying saucers in case I didn't tell you.

1. Do you think the example paragraph has good rhythm?

_____ Why? _____

_____

2. What, if anything is wrong with the example paragraph?

_____

_____

Besides having no rhythm and long sentences, the paragraph also has *run-on sentences.* Run-ons happen when two sentences are incorrectly combined. Look at the run-on sentence and its corrections below.

Run-on: The alarm rang I jumped up.
Correct: The alarm rang, and I jumped up.

B. Now rewrite the paragraph on the lines below using different sentence lengths. Also, make any run-on sentences two or more complete sentences.

_____

_____

_____

_____

_____

_____

_____

_____

_____

Sometimes, writing suffers from another problem. Instead of being too long, sentences are too short or choppy.

The alarm rang. It was seven. I jumped up.

The way to avoid choppiness is to *vary* the kinds of sentences you use—some short ones, some longer ones.

 Get out the paragraph you wrote for Lesson 2, persuading the reader to swallow a spoonful of vinegar. Can you make improvements that will make the paragraph flow more smoothly? If so, rewrite it. (If its rhythm is already good, rewrite a Write On paragraph from some other lesson in this unit.)

Rhythm makes writing interesting and smooth. Make sure your writing has rhythm.

Proofreading

Using past tense verbs

Osmond jumps high. Osmond jumped high.

A. Read the sentences above. Then write answers to the following questions.

1. What are the verbs in the sentences?

   _____   _____

2. Which sentence, the first or the second, tells what is happening *now?* _____

3. Which sentence tells what has *already happened?*

   _____

   Verbs that tell what has already happened are in the **past tense** form. Most verbs in the past tense end with **-d** or **-ed.**

B. Read the sentences below. Then write the past tense form of the verbs given.

1. Julie <u>watches</u> the parade. _____

2. Ted <u>calls</u> his horse. _____

3. He <u>walks</u> quickly. _____

4. They <u>play</u> hard. _____

5. Sheila <u>dances</u> beautifully. _____

Some verbs don't add -*d* or -*ed* to form their past tense. Instead they change spelling. For example: *fly—flew, take—took, drink—drank.* If you are not sure of how the past tense of a verb is spelled, look it up in your dictionary.

C. Read the sentences below. Then write the past tense form for each verb given.

1. Coreen <u>drinks</u> lots of fruit punch. _____

2. Robert <u>flies</u> his model airplane. _____

3. Barbara <u>leaves</u> early in the day. _____

4. Jason <u>runs</u> fast. _____

5. We <u>go</u> to a basketball game. _____

To form the past tense, most verbs end with -<u>d</u> or -<u>ed</u>.
To form the past tense, some verbs change spelling.

---

1. Read the paragraph below. Decide if the purpose is to inform, persuade, or entertain. Then cross out the sentences that don't fit the purpose.

      Penguins are flightless birds that live in Antarctica. They have flipperlike wings and stiff, oily feathers. What's black and white and black and white? The answer is penguins rolling down a hill. Penguins are awkward on land, but they are very good swimmers.

Purpose:_____

2. Circle the words you could use to persuade someone that ice cream is not good for you.

    sticky   fattening   flavorful   tooth-decaying

    creamy   sickly-sweet   drippy   lip-smacking good

3. Write a paragraph that would inform a new student about your school.

4. Break this sentence into smaller sentences to improve the rhythm.

      Jacky and I went to the zoo early so it wouldn't be too crowded and we saw a baby polar bear and some young giraffes and then we had lunch at the zoo restaurant.

5. Rewrite these sentences so that the choppy rhythm becomes smoother.

      Jeff called. He forgot his notebook. I gave him the history assignment. We chatted awhile.

unit 8
Point of View in Writing

Things to Remember About Point of View in Your Writing

A **point of view** is how someone sees and thinks about something.

Writing

- Decide on your point of view before you begin to write.
- Write with honest feeling to make your writing more interesting.
- Use an unusual point of view sometimes.
- Use only one point of view at a time.

Revising and Proofreading Tips

Check to see whether your paragraph
- says exactly what you want it to say
- could use rewriting

1 Writing from different points of view

Think about an ear of corn. Here's what a scientist might say about it:

"Hmm . . . not a bad-looking specimen of *zea mays* if I do say so. Hybrid, unless I miss my guess, and apparently grown with potash-enriched fertilizer."

Now consider what a shopper in a supermarket might say about the same ear of corn:

"Thirty cents an ear? Oh my, the prices are terrible these days. Oh well, it looks about the right size for our cookpot, and tomorrow, if there's some left over, I'll mix it with the left-over lima beans and we'll have succotash."

Both speakers were looking at the same thing—an ear of corn. But their different **points of view** caused them to think completely different things about it. A point of view is how someone sees and thinks about something.

A. On the lines below, try writing from a different point of view. Write about the ear of corn from the point of view of a small corn-borer worm inside one of the kernels.

_____

_____

_____

_____

_____

B. Look at the picture below. Then write two short paragraphs about it. Write the first one from the point of view of an artist painting a picture. Write the second one from the point of view of a woodpecker.

An artist: _____

_____

_____

_____

A woodpecker: _____

_____

_____

_____

 On another sheet of paper, write two paragraphs about the Pilgrims' landing on Plymouth Rock — from the <u>point</u> <u>of</u> <u>view</u> <u>of</u> <u>the</u> <u>rock</u>.

How you write depends on your point of view.

2 Writing with feeling

A. When you look at the jack-o'-lantern above, it might make you think of the fun and excitement of trick-or-treating. Write a paragraph about the jack-o'-lantern that expresses that exciting, pleasant mood.

_____

_____

_____

_____

B. On the other hand, the picture might make you think sadly of the coming of winter or fearfully of ghosts and the unknown. Write a paragraph about the jack-o-lantern expressing a different mood.

_____

_____

_____

_____

C. Look at the scoreboard at the end of the big basketball game between the Lynxes and the Leapers:

LYNXES   LEAPERS
104   78

1. Pretend you're one of the <u>Lynxes</u> and write a paragraph from the winner's point of view.

_____

_____

_____

_____

2. Now pretend you're one of the <u>Leapers</u> and write a paragraph from the losing point of view.

_____

_____

_____

_____

_____

On another sheet of paper, write two paragraphs about hearing the alarm clock go off — one on an average day, the other on a day when you're going to the circus.

Writing with honest feeling makes writing more interesting.

lesson 3 Writing a story from a point of view

Look at the people in the picture.

MOVIE DIRECTOR   FOREST RANGER   NEWSPAPER REPORTER

Below is the story of "Goldilocks," as told by one of the people in the picture.

"According to reports from other campers, the subject—one Goldilocks—left Big Meadow campsite, hiking west on Grizzly Trail at about 2 p.m. In spite of the numerous "Stay Away From Bears" signs that we have posted around the park, the subject went into a den occupied by two adult bears and one cub. The subject escaped unharmed but deposited a pile of litter, including some damaged furniture and several spilled bowls of porridge. I recommend that a warning letter be sent to the subject by the National Parks Commission."

A. Write answers to the questions below.

   1. Which person probably told the story?

_____

   2. Why do you think it is that person? _____

_____

B. Now try to tell "Goldilocks" from the viewpoint of one of the other people in the picture. First say who you are and then write the story.

_____

_____

_____

_____

_____

_____

_____

_____

Write On

On another sheet of paper rewrite the story of "Snow White and the Seven Dwarfs" as told from the point of view of the wicked witch. Or you may think of a different story to rewrite from another point of view. In either case make sure you give the title of the story and tell from whose point of view the story is being told.

Every story has a point of view.

Writing about an event as one person sees it

Look at the picture below.

A. Write about what is shown in the picture from the point of view of one of the people.

_____

_____

_____

_____

_____

_____

_____

B. Now choose one of the people in the picture on this page, and write about the scene from that person's point of view.

_____

_____

_____

_____

_____

_____

 On another sheet of paper write a paragraph about someone making scrambled eggs. Write from the point of view of one of the eggs. Make your paragraph at least five sentences long.

Different people sometimes see the same thing with different points of view.

Revising and Proofreading

Rewriting

You already know that *proofreading* means reading over your work and correcting any errors it may have. Along with proofreading your writing, you may often have to **rewrite** it. Rewriting means improving your writing. You may want to use more exact nouns, verbs, or adjectives. Or you may want to put better rhythm in your writing by changing the length of your sentences. Or you just may want to make your writing clearer.

A. Read the following paragraph. Then read the "rewrite" of the same paragraph below. Finally write answers to the questions that follow.

It was a good day. The sun was out. The air was nice. The trees moved in the wind. I felt very nice.

Saturday was a delicious fall day. The sun was bright, and the air was crisp and clear. The trees rustled leaf-songs. I felt as excited as the flaming colors of red, yellow, and orange.

1. What is one more exact noun that is used in the rewrite?

_____

2. What more exact verb is used? _____

_____

3. What more exact adjectives are used? _____

_____

4. Write the first three words of the two sentences that are

combined. _____

5.   Do you think the rewrite is an improvement? _____

     Why? _____

B. Do your own rewrite of the next paragraph on the lines below. Look back at the rewrite in part A if you need help.

     She got up one morning. She got dressed. She had breakfast. She went outside. She played all afternoon.

_____

_____

_____

_____

_____

 Now find one paragraph that you have written for this unit that could use rewriting. On another sheet of paper, rewrite that paragraph. Think about sentence length, exact nouns, verbs, and adjectives. Ask yourself if your paragraph says exactly what you want it to say.

Rewrite to improve your writing.

Post-Test

1. Read the paragraph below. Underline the choice that best describes the point of view of the paragraph.

> I couldn't wait for 6:30 a.m. The thought of it kept me ticking all night long. What fun it would be to wake up the entire family with the sound of my voice!

   a. a man who has to catch the 7:15 a.m. train
   b. a new alarm clock set for 6:30
   c. a baby who cries frequently during the night

2. Read the following paragraphs and think about their points of view.

   A. Our new house was big but run-down. It would take a lot of work repairing the walls and controlling the mice.
   B. The new house couldn't be better! There are plenty of holes for me to hide in and enough mice to keep me off that canned stuff for a year!

   a. Whose point of view could paragraph A express?

   _____

   b. Whose point of view could paragraph B express?

   _____

3. Write a paragraph about a summer picnic from the point of view of a mosquito.

4. Rewrite the following paragraph so that it flows more smoothly. You may add more exact or interesting words.

   The street fair was big. It was jammed. Ted walked through.

   He sampled a sausage here, a sandwich there and listened to a

   country band with a nice singer and bought five records.

124

Answer Key

Unit 1

Lesson 1 (pages 2–3)

A. Meats
lamb chops   chicken   hamburger
Fruits
lemons   cherries   bananas
Cleaning Aids
soap powder   furniture polish
window cleaner

B. Fish   **Money**   **Trees**
trout, etc.   quarter, etc.   birch, etc.

C. Candy
lollipops   lemon drops   ~~onions~~
jelly beans
Birds
canary   ~~cat~~   rooster   sparrow
Sports
skating   swimming   basketball
~~arithmetic~~

Lesson 2 (pages 4–5)

A. You should have underlined 2.
B. You might have said:
People are throwing tomatoes.
People are walking out.
People are making faces.
C. You should have underlined 3.
D. Details: The car wouldn't start.
    Two angry customers were waiting.
    He got a headache.
    His favorite TV show wasn't on.
Main Idea: Mr. Montez had a terrible day.

Lesson 3 (pages 6–7)

A. 1. She was the prettiest horse I ever saw.
    2. You should have written two of these details:
    Her hide shone like a copper kettle.
    Her tail streamed in the breeze.
    She tossed her head proudly.
B. You should have underlined these sentences:
Julio got to the basement without making a sound.
But I think rainy days can be fun.
C. You might have said:
It was the hottest day of the year.

Lesson 4 (pages 8–9)

A. the police officer and the stoplight
B. 1. You should have underlined:
What an exciting game we played last Saturday!
You should have crossed out:
She has red hair.

---

    2. You should have underlined:
The band members were getting ready to play.
You should have crossed out:
Tickets to the band concert were quite expensive.
    3. You should have underlined:
Uncle Jake loves to make unusual sandwiches.
You should have crossed out:
Did you ever watch a monkey eat a banana?

Lesson 5 (pages 10–11)

A. ⇨ Whenever you see this symbol, check with your teacher.
B. ⇨

Lesson 6 (pages 12–13)

A. ⇨
B. Here are some examples:
    1. Bird: robin, sparrow, parrot
    2. Color: red, yellow, brown
    3. Flower: rose, tulip, lily
    4. Sport: baseball, swimming, tennis
    5. Vegetable: corn, peas, spinach
    6. Building: barn, apartment house, cottage
    7. Furniture: table, desk, sofa
C. You should have circled:
    1. barn   2. horses   3. carrot
D. ⇨

Lesson 7 (pages 14–15)

A. 1. NS   2. S   3. NS
    4. NS   5. S
B. Do you like to fly? I think planes are great. They can fly you all over the world in just a few hours. How I wish I were on a plane right now!

Unit 2

Lesson 1 (pages 18–19)

A. Did you show the girl landing on the other side of the hedge?
B. First the girl ran toward the hedge.
Next the girl jumped over the hedge.
Last the girl landed on the other side.
C. last   first   next
D. First the boy was given an ice cream cone.
Next he started to eat the cone.
Last the ice cream fell out of the cone.

Lesson 2 (pages 20–21)

A. You should have underlined:
first, then, Next, Finally
B. Your sequence words may be different, but your sentence order should be:
First Lester LeMouche peered at his pocket watch and saw that it was dinner time. Next he showered and shaved. Then he got dressed. After that, he splashed aftershave on his jaw and threaded a rosebud through the buttonhole in his jacket. Finally, the elegant Lester LeMouche strolled down the avenue to his favorite restaurant.

125

Lesson 3 (pages 22–23)

A. First, turn off the alarm.
Second, get out of bed.
Third, Fourth, Fifth—The order may be different.
Last, put on a coat.

B. ▷

Lesson 4 (pages 24–25)

A. 5   4   6   1   3   2

B. ▷

Lesson 5 (pages 26–27)

A. You should have written the numerals in this order: 2, 4, 1, 5, 3

B. ▷

Lesson 6 (pages 28–29)

A. You might have said:
1. whispered, shouted
2. gobbled, chewed
3. strolled, trudged
4. drove, flew
5. patted, kicked

B. ▷

Lesson 7 (pages 30–31)

A. 1. Thanksgiving Day, Wednesday
2. Rex, Mickey Mouse
3. California, Atlanta

B. ▷

C. 1. opossums   2. women   3. ponies
4. feet   5. pitches   6. hammocks
7. boxes   8. deer

Unit 3

Lesson 1 (pages 34–35)

A. 1. The cow on the left is fatter.
2. The sneaker on the right is cleaner.

B. You might have chosen these adjectives:
1. bigger   2. more playful
3. faster, more expensive 4. deeper, bigger
5. brighter, bigger

Lesson 2 (pages 36–37)

A. ▷   **B.** ▷

Lesson 3 (pages 38–39)

A. You should have underlined:
most interesting, lowest, most magnificent, most mysterious

B. 1. shorter   2. more   3. biggest

C. 1. better   2. best   3. worse
4. worst

Lesson 4 (pages 40–41)

A. 1. stomach and doughnut hole
2. stage and fireflies

B. ▷   **C.** ▷

Lesson 5 (pages 42–43)

A. ▷   **B.** ▷

126

Lesson 6 (pages 44–45)

A. 1. bitter   2. vicious   3. icy
4. honest   5. sunny   6. mysterious
7. magnificent

B. correct—right   awkward—clumsy
lucky—fortunate   little—tiny
odd—peculiar

C. ▷

Lesson 7 (pages 46–47)

A. 1. statements and commands
2. question   3. exclamation

B. 1. What a tall building that is!
2. How many floors does it have?
3. It is the tallest building in the world. (or !)
4. Can we go to the top?
5. Push the button for the elevator.
6. Here it comes. (or !)
7. Whee! This is fun!
8. Are we at the top yet?

C. 1. Do you like to ski, Lester?
2. Yes, Jackie, I do.
3. I like skiing, skating, and tennis.
4. Sports provide good, healthful exercise.

D. The pond was a cool, silvery mirror. People skimmed, twirled, and bumped to the ground. The sounds of laughter and shouting filled the crisp air. Was it a grand ball at the palace? No, it was only Cooper Lake in the ice-skating season.

Unit 4

Lesson 1 (pages 50–51)

A. You should have underlined:
old, spotted; limping slowly; dirt road; thick hair; caked with dust; tired animal; giant maple tree; thick patch of grass.
You should have checked picture 2.

B. You might have listed:
girl crouching, suit with stars and stripes, white bathing cap, platform, pool, starter with gun raised looking at watch

C ▷

Lesson 2 (pages 52–53)

A. You should have crossed out:
Someone came in the back door and slammed it.
The dark gold color of the counter top shined.

B. You should have put an X next to:
crisp peanut butter coating
thick and crunchy
filled with coconut and honey
colorfully wrapped
bite-size pieces

Lesson 3 (pages 54–55)

A. You should have at least one answer for each:
a porcupine's sharp spines—touch, sight
puffy clouds—sight
a creaking door—hearing
a turkey roasting—smell, sight
a silk shirt—touch, sight

peppery sausage—taste, smell
birds chirping—hearing
B.

Lesson 4 (pages 56–57)
A. 1. ice cream   2. a clock
B.
C. 1. a potato   2. a comb   3. a clock

Lesson 5 (pages 58–59)
A.   **B.**

Lesson 6 (pages 60–61)
A.
B. 1. alertly   2. cautiously   3. fortunately
    4. quickly   5. angrily   6. easily
C.

Lesson 7 (pages 62–63)
A. digs hunts gather cook
B. 1. gather and cook   2. digs and hunts
C. 1. runs   2. buys   3. like   4. look
    5. tastes   6. seem   7. hides
D.

Unit 5

Lesson 1 (pages 66–67)
A. Mom and Dad brought home my new bike yesterday. F
It has racing stripes and a handlebar-mounted gearshift. F
I think it would easily beat Eddie Blaine's bike in a race. O
I bet it cost a lot more than Eddie's too. O
Dad didn't tell me exactly how much my bike cost. F
But I think it's the best-looking bike on the block. O
B.   **C.**

Lesson 2 (pages 68–69)
A. 1. fact   2. opinion   3. fact
    4. opinion   5. opinion
B.

Lesson 3 (pages 70–71)
A. You should have underlined:
On the way to school I found a dollar.
I took it to the school office.
The secretary told me that if nobody claimed it I could have it at 3 o'clock.
Finally 3 o'clock arrived.
The secretary smiled and handed me the bill, saying, "Nobody claimed it."
On the way home I bought two comics.
You should have circled:
Today was pretty lucky.
I think it must have fallen out of somebody's pocket.
I felt nervous when I went into the office.
I felt great.

B.   **C.**

Lesson 4 (pages 72–73)
A. 1. running   2. New York
    3. 26 miles   4. No. It was too warm.
B.

Lesson 5 (pages 74–75)
A. 1. But the whole stalk was growing so quickly that the boy couldn't get down.
    2. You might have written one of the first two sentences or "He called for help and his neighbor came running with an ax."
    3. They shot food up with a cannon.

Lesson 6 (pages 76–77)
A. Billy; Mark
B. You should have underlined <u>painted the fence</u> and <u>cleaned the yard.</u>
C. 1. Carla called Ralph and waved to Ann.
    2. Maxine and Sylvia arrived at 6 o'clock.
    3. Susan and Karen walked three miles today.
    4. Rodney reads and writes a lot.
    5. Duncan jumped out of bed and ran down the stairs.
    6. The tiny squirrel peeped from behind the tree and scurried away.
    7. The class ended and was dismissed.
    8. Fryma prepared and served dinner.

Lesson 7 (pages 78–79)
A. 1. year; city   2. April 23, 1967
    3. city
B. 1. Dover, Delaware   2. July 20, 1969
    3. Avenue, Bangor, Maine
C.

Unit 6

Lesson 1 (pages 82–83)
A. The nails dropped out of a hole in the man's pocket.
B. 1. c   2. a   3. d   4. b
C.

Lesson 2 (pages 84–85)
A. You should have underlined:
Since, As a result, because of, Due to the fact that, Therefore
B. 1. because   2. so; therefore
    3. Since; Because; Due to the fact that
    4. So; Therefore; As a result
C. You might have said:
Since the boy knocked over the bowling bag, the ball fell out. The noised frightened the cat and caused it to jump into the woman's lap. As a result, the women threw up her hands and the newspapers were scattered.

Lesson 3 (pages 86–87)
A. 1. the snow

2. You should have listed three of these effects:
Children missed school.
Many businesses had to close.
Some people began to run low on food.
Snowmobile sellers, skiers, and others were happy.

B. ➥

Lesson 4 (pages 88–89)

A. You should have written an X next to number 2.

B. ➥

Lesson 5 (pages 90–91)

A. Who: The Fish Fanciers Club of Mackerel
What: They held a festival.
When: March 18
Where: at the town dock in Mackerel
Why: They wanted to get people to understand the importance of fish.

B. ➥

Lesson 6 (pages 92–93)

A. 1. The nervous patient   2. The eager dentist
3. The painful tooth

B. 1. The nervous patient clutched his chair.
2. The eager dentist grabbed her tools.
3. The painful tooth was soon out.

C. The black cat howled on the back fence. The angry man threw his shoe at the cat. That woke everyone up.

Lesson 7 (pages 94–95)

A. 1. an apostrophe and an *s*   2. an apostrophe

B. 1. the baby's cocoa
2. the musicians' instruments
3. the fans' yells
4. the fire fighter's boots
5. the teachers' room

C. 1. o   2. wi   3. i

D. 1. couldn't   2. aren't   3. I'll
4. they'll   5. she's   6. it's

E. 1. Isn't, Alan's   2. He's
3. Doesn't, actors'

Unit 7

Lesson 1 (pages 98–99)

A. 1. persuade   2. entertain   3. inform

B. ➥

Lesson 2 (pages 100–101)

A. 2

B. 1. It's a super day.
2. I bet you can hit the ball farther than you ever did before with this bat.
3. Maybe we can get a soda afterward.

C. ➥

Lesson 3 (pages 102–103)

A. You should have underlined:
springtime-fresh, enjoyment, bright, happy, laughter, lovingly

B. You should have underlined:

Fire, damage, grim, terrible, ruined, lose, sick, sad, broke

C. ➥

Lesson 4 (pages 104–105)

A. 1. the complete plant catalogue
2. the left side
3. the sender's address and the date
4. Sincerely   5. Dear Raoul
6. a colon (:)   7. the body

Lesson 5 (pages 106–107)

A. 1. Yes, the reviewer gives a short summary of the plot in the first paragraph.
2. The reviewer thinks the book is bad.
3. a. There is not enough information about Arthur.
b. We don't know Arthur's feelings and can't tell about the ending.

B. ➥

Lesson 6 (pages 108–109)

A. 1. No—the sentences are all too long.
2. The sentences run on without the correct punctuation.
The thoughts are not organized into clear sentences.

B. ➥

Lesson 7 (pages 110–111)

A. 1. jumps   jumped
2. the first   3. the second

B. 1. watched   2. called   3. walked
4. played   5. danced

C. 1. drank   2. flew   3. left
4. ran   5. went

Unit 8

Lesson 1 (pages 114–115)

A. ➥   B. ➥

Lesson 2 (pages 116–117)

A. ➥   B. ➥   C. ➥

Lesson 3 (pages 118–119)

A. 1. The Forest Ranger
2. He talks about campers, the park, and the National Parks Commission.

B. ➥

Lesson 4 (pages 120–121)

A. ➥   B. ➥

Lesson 5 (pages 122–123)

A. 1. You might have said *leaf-songs* or *colors*.
2. rustled
3. delicious, bright, crisp, clear, excited, flaming
4. The sun was
5. Yes. More exact words are used; the rhythm is better; a simile makes the writing more colorful

B. ➥

Post-Test Answers; pg 16

1. a. wrench   b. billboard
2. Underline sentence: Toga seemed to know it was the first day of spring.
3. b.
4. The topic sentence should appear in the student's paragraph, preferably as the first or last sentence. Make sure that the five other sentences in the paragraph support the main idea.
5. Mom finished third in the minimarathon. We cheered her at the finish line. <u>She has been</u> (or similar words) only running for one year.

Post-Test Answers; pg 32

1. 2, 1, 4, 3
2. Students' paragraphs may vary slightly. They should add the two steps that were left out: buying the movie tickets (after sentence 1) and buying the popcorn (after sentence 2). Check to see that the sequence is clear and that sequence words are added.
3. Answers will vary. Possible answers:
   a. sneaked, slinked, crept, prowled
   b. pounced, leaped, sprang, lunged
4. a. Jamie visited <u>U</u>ncle <u>N</u>ed in <u>O</u>klahoma <u>C</u>ity.
   b. We needed two box<u>es</u> to put all the game<u>s</u> away.

Post-Test Answers; pg 48

1. a. higher   c. more curious
   b. most beautiful
2. Answers will vary. Possible answers:
   a. The alarm clock rang like a dentist's drill.
   b. The new sports car was as sleek as a cat.
3. Answers will vary. Make sure that students have used -er and more correctly with comparative adjectives. Each sentence in the paragraph should contribute to the comparison.
4. a. husky
   b. tangy
   c. blistering
5. <u>D</u>id you ever hear of an outer-space greeting card<u>?</u> Many spaceships contain tapes<u>,</u> pictures<u>,</u> and other objects from Earth<u>.</u> Scientists hope that intelligent beings will find these spaceships.

Post-Test Answers; pg 64

1. Crossed-out sentence: I play softball there after school.
2. Answers will vary. Make sure that the details convey a taste, sight, smell, sound and touch.
3. Be sure that the detail sentences in the students' paragraphs are related to the main idea of a Thanksgiving dinner. The sentences should use the information given in Exercise 2, as well as any additional details.
4. a. goes   b. shed   c. plays

Post-Test Answers; pg 80

1. F, O, F, F, O
2. Answers will vary. Answers should reflect students' awareness that a fact is a true, provable statement, while an opinion is not. You may wish to have students underline opinion clue words.
3. a. Chrissy and Ken built a sand monster.
   b. The elephant raised its trunk and roared.
4. The opinion expressed in the paragraphs will vary. Students should use clue words like *think, worst, hate,* although they are not strictly necessary.

Post-Test Answers; pg 96

1. a. because   b. therefore
2. b.
3. Answers will vary. Possible answers:
   where: They were off the coast of Florida.
   when: It happened on June 23.
4. Students' paragraphs should have five effects clearly related to a power failure in town. The paragraph should begin with a topic sentence stating the cause.

Post-Test Answers; pg 112

1. Crossed-out sentences: What's black and white and black and white? The answer is penguins rolling down a hill.
   Purpose: to inform
2. Circled words: sticky, fattening, sickly sweet, drippy, tooth-decaying
3. Students' paragraphs should be largely factual. The purpose of the paragraphs should be to *inform*, not persuade or entertain.
4. Jacky and I went to the zoo early so it wouldn't be too crowded. We saw a baby polar bear and some young giraffes.
   Then we had lunch at the zoo restaurant.
5. Answers may vary slightly. Possible answer: Jeff called because he forgot his notebook. I gave him the history assignment, and then we chatted awhile.

Post-Test Answers; pg 124

1. b.
2. Answers may vary slightly. Possible answers:
   a. the people who bought the house
   b. a cat who lives with the family
3. Be sure that students' paragraphs express the point of view of a mosquito. The point of view may be stated directly or implied through details.
4. Answers may vary, but students should note that the first three sentences are choppy and the fourth sentence is a run-on. Possible answer:

   The street fair was big and jammed with strollers. Ted wandered through and sampled a sausage at one food booth and a sandwich at another. He listened to a country band with a fresh, new singer. Then he bought five country records.